Drafting Plus

5 Simple Steps to Pattern Drafting and More!

Sharyn Squier Craig

CHITRA PUBLICATIONS

Chitra Publications
2 Public Avenue
Montrose, Pennsylvania 18801

First printing: 1994

Library of Congress Cataloging-in-Publication Data.

Craig, Sharyn Squier, 1947-
    Drafting plus: 5 simple steps to pattern drafting and more!
/ by Sharyn Squier Craig.

        p. cm.
    Includes bibliographical references.
    ISBN 0-9622565-4-4 : $14.95
    1. Patchwork--Patterns   2. Patchwork quilts.   I. Title.
TT835.C733 1994
746.46'041--dc20   94-5637
                                              CIP

Editors: Pamela Moss Watts
              Patti Lilik Bachelder
Design and Illustration: Mark D. Wayman
Photography: Stephen J. Appel Photography,
 Vestal, New York
Portrait Photo by: Ken Jacques Photography,
National City, California

Acknowledgements

Special thanks go to the following people for their roles in helping this book become a reality. Without their support and encouragement, it wouldn't have happened!

To my first quilting teacher, Bobbie Winkelman, who didn't give me a choice whether or not to learn drafting— it was the only way we could get pattern pieces to make quilts!

To all of my adult education students, who also had to participate in drafting classes if they wanted to make quilts. Without those classes, I wouldn't have learned as much about the subject and how to teach it.

To Linda Hamby, my student and friend, who gave of herself and her time whenever I called for help.

To Christiane Meunier, my publisher, who sat in my sewing room and said, "What book do you want to write? I want to publish it." Without her insistence, none of this would have happened.

To my editor, Pam, to Patti and all the rest of the technical staff at Chitra Publications, for their understanding, patience, insight and hours of work on this text.

But most especially, to my husband George, my number one priority, who has unselfishly made it possible for me to have a fabulous marriage and a satisfying career.

Thank you all!

Sharyn

Dedication

I dedicate this book to quilters everywhere who want their quilts to be unique. The information found on these pages can unlock the doors to creative freedom. Without a simple understanding of patchwork block structure, we're forever dependent on someone else's pattern. With knowledge comes freedom, and with that freedom comes the satisfaction of knowing your quilts are special!

Contents

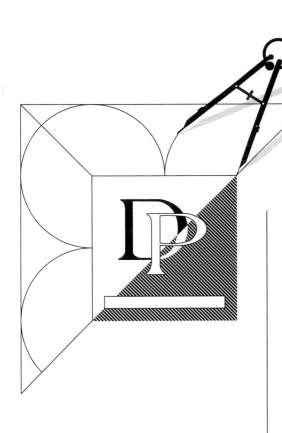

Introduction

INTRO

My first book, *Designing New Traditions in Quilts*, was meant to open the doors to creativity through visual stimulation and show you how to work beyond duplication. But I knew that, without the power to understand the patchwork block structure, all the creative license in the world wouldn't enable you to actually become creative. This book will allow you to do that.

Drafting Plus is a reality because of the positive reactions to my column "Drafting Plus" in *Traditional Quiltworks* magazine. Much of this material appeared in the magazine during the two years after the publication of my first book. Readers liked what they read but did not like searching through back issues for a particular installment or the occasional misplaced issue. In answer to their requests, all of the information has been re-edited and is presented here in one easy-to-read book.

In my travels around the country teaching creativity in quilting, I have found that a tremendous volume of patterns for quilts and quilt blocks has become available in recent years. This has resulted in what I call "recipe" quilting—following other people's designs and patterns. Following someone else's directions can be a great introduction to quilting. As you gain more experience, however, you will enjoy knowing that you can create your own special, one-of-a-kind quilts by drafting your own patterns. My goal in writing this book is to enable you to create any patchwork block you want to make, in any size you desire.

Growing up, I was lucky to have teachers who did more than just teach me facts. They taught me how to think for myself. For example, I recall not being able to spell the word ketchup. When I asked the teacher how to spell it, she looked at me and exclaimed, "What a great question!" Instead of spelling the word for me, she took the time to teach me how to use a dictionary. She worked with me to sound out the word. In the end, of course, we came up with two possibilities for spelling that word—ketchup or catsup. Either was right, so I could make my own choice. That teacher gave me so much more than just an answer to my question. I learned a skill-building technique, developed the self-confidence to find my own solutions, and learned to make choices.

I want you to learn how to make choices in the quilts you make by being in control of all aspects of quilt design. The number of blocks you will use, their size and the size of the finished quilt is up to you. *You* decide if the quilt should have borders and if so, how wide, etc. Your quilts can become expressions of your individuality.

There are some excellent technique books on the market today. I encourage you to use these books, and to take as many classes and workshops as you can. Be open-minded. The material presented here is the way I work. I offer it as guidelines, not rules. New quilters may be frustrated hearing different professional quilters' opinions on the same subject, especially when each teacher is dogmatic about why she prefers one way over another. How do you determine whom to believe? Try everything. Then decide which techniques work best for you. When you understand the "how-to," think about the potential for creative freedom. When you see a quilt you like, it's hard not to copy it exactly. But wouldn't it be more personally satisfying to make a quilt that is yours and yours alone?

So, where do you start? First, stop thinking of the word "draft" as a four-letter word. After all, it isn't! There is no mystery and you don't need a mathematics degree. If our pioneer ancestors could make such beautiful quilts without being mathematicians, so can you! The key to successful pattern drafting is understanding basic patchwork structure. I think you will be pleasantly surprised at how simple this process is, and you will gain confidence in yourself as a creative quilter.

There are five simple steps to patchwork pattern drafting.

1) Identify the base grid.
2) Determine the block size.
3) Identify the pattern pieces needed.
4) Determine the finished size of the pattern pieces.
5) Create the templates.

Many quilters do not want to work with templates, so methods for working without templates are discussed in Chapter 4. Note that working without templates requires more math, and also that using templates does not mean you can't use a rotary cutter. Because I prefer to use templates, I have devoted a whole section to creating them and will show you how to use the rotary cutter with a template. As a bonus, you will also learn how to care for your rotary cutter properly.

On the following pages, each of the five steps will be explained fully, with sample exercises to guide you. Chances are that, later on, you will need only this list to remind you of what to do.

Welcome to the world of creative freedom in quilting. And remember—knowledge is freedom!

How to Use This Book

The easiest way to approach the information in this book is to begin by gathering the supplies recommended for drafting. In the back of the book there are sample sheets of graph paper for you to experiment with. If you can't find accurate graph paper, turn to page 78 for information on how to order graph paper or any of the other recommended supplies.

Next, read from the beginning and do all the exercises. This book is your workbook. Write in it. Record your responses to the exercises in the margins and sketch your ideas as they come to you. Draft the templates suggested in the Master Templates list, even if you don't think you will ever use them. Trying it now will make it easier later if you should ever need templates for a particular block. And understanding pattern drafting will make quilting without templates easier to understand, too.

It should take only a few hours to complete all the exercises and make the Master Templates. Pay careful attention to the section on storing templates. Nothing is more frustrating than knowing you have those templates somewhere and not being able to find them!

Finally, decide whether you want to work with or without templates. Then choose a block from one of the exercises or from the Sample Blocks appendix and start cutting fabric! After all, the main reason we got into this in the first place was to make quilts—so what are you waiting for?

Whether you decide to make a sampler quilt or a repeating block quilt, or use the blocks in another way, you will soon discover the joy of being able to create *your own* beautiful quilts.

 ## Pattern Drafting Supplies

Graph Paper

Accurate graph paper is a must for drafting accurate patterns. I recommend Engineering Forms paper by National®. Regular 1/4" (4 squares to the inch) graph paper is used most often. However, you will find that graph paper in 5, 6, 8 and 10 squares to the inch is also valuable. Which size paper to use is determined by the particular needs of your design.

A variety of graph paper is available to quilters. On some, the lines are darker at 1" intervals, making it easier to work with. The 1/8" and 1/4" graph papers are useful for marking 1/4" seam allowances. On other graph paper, you'll need a ruler to add accurate 1/4" seam allowances.

To decide which graph paper is appropriate for your particular needs, analyze the size(s) of your pattern pieces. If the size is a whole number, a whole number plus 1/2", or a whole number plus 1/4", standard 1/4" graph paper will work successfully. For other sizes, choose the appropriate number of squares per inch. For example, a pattern piece that finishes at 2 1/8" is easy to draft on graph paper with eight squares to the inch. In the same manner a 2 2/5" pattern piece is simple to draft on graph paper with 5 squares to the inch.

Ruler

I recommend the 2" x 18" C-Thru® ruler for pattern drafting. This clear plastic ruler is marked with red grid lines every 1/8" in both directions. It is also available in 1" x 6", 1" x 12" and 2" x 18" sizes. It is important to note that all rulers are a little bit different. Become comfortable with one ruler and then use it exclusively. It is also a good idea to use the same long edge of the ruler each time, since the distance between the red line and the edge can vary from one side of the ruler to the other. Mark your favorite side with permanent pen or a dot of nail polish.

Pencils and Erasers

Sharp pencils and good erasers are invaluable drafting tools. I don't recommend thick lead because as it wears down line widths vary, causing inaccuracies in pattern pieces. Many people prefer mechanical pencils because they consistently make fine lines.

Template Plastic

Look for clear heavyweight plastic with *no grids*.

Buy the stiffest plastic than can still be cut with household scissors.

Sandpaper

Buy heavyweight, fine-to-medium grit sandpaper. I prefer the black wet/dry variety, which has a finer grain and heavier paper stock.

Glue Stick

Glue sticks can be purchased at quilt shops, office supply stores, art supply stores and grocery stores. The Dennison™ glue stick works particularly well.

Protractor

A protractor is used for drawing and measuring angles. It is essential for drafting fan blocks.

Compass

A compass is used for drawing arcs or circles and taking measurements. It, too, is essential for drafting fan blocks.

Other Supplies

You will also need paper-cutting scissors, a hand-held calculator and removable tape.

NOTE: *The Quilter's Treasure Box offers a Starter Drafting Kit that includes John Flynn's Cut-Your-Own Templates kit with template material and cutting shears; one C-Thru 2" x 18" ruler; and an 80-sheet package of graph paper in 6 sizes (20 each of 1/4", 1/5", 1/6", 1/7", 1/8" and 1/10" sizes). Turn to page 78 for ordering information.* ◢

Drafting Grid Blocks

1. Identify the Base Grid

The *base grid* of a block consists of horizontal and vertical lines that intersect at equal intervals across the block, resulting in a checkerboard-like grid. Most patchwork designs are created when triangles, squares and other shapes are superimposed over this basic underlying structure. (Some patchwork patterns, such as eight-pointed stars and fan blocks, fall into a different category. We'll discuss these later.)

The following diagrams illustrate some of the most common base grids. Terms such as 9-patch, 4-patch, 5-patch or 7-patch mean that the number of equal divisions in the block will be a multiple of that number. For example, you might find 9 equal divisions in a 9-patch block, or possibly 36 equal divisions—both are divisible by the number 9. The same holds true for other blocks as well; e.g., a 4-patch block could consist of 4 equal divisions in the block, or some other multiple of 4, like 16, or 64, as shown in the following diagrams.

COMMON BASE GRIDS

9-patch

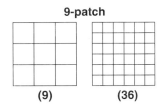

(9)   (36)

4-patch

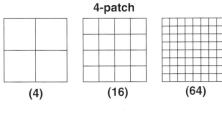

(4)   (16)   (64)

5-patch   7-patch

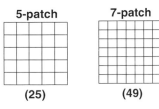

(25)   (49)

The lines of the base grid may not be visible in the design of the finished block. Some shapes used in

a quilt block may be larger or smaller than one of the equal divisions in the underlying grid. The Puss in the Corner block is a good example of this.

Puss in the Corner

4-Patch

Let's look at some quilt blocks and learn to identify their underlying base grids. Look at each block carefully. How many equal divisions are there across and down each block? Remember, the underlying grid is not necessarily visible in the block design.

Double X

Base grid has 3 equal units across and down (9-patch).
In this block, all grid lines are visible.

Whirligig

Base grid has 4 equal units across and down (4-patch). The dashes reveal the underlying grid,which is not visible in the design itself.

Wrench

Base grid has 5 equal units across and down (5-patch). The middle section of this block makes it easy to spot the 5 equal units.

Bear's Paw

Base grid has 7 equal units across and down (7-patch). The grid can be easily recognized by counting the units along one side of the block.

Now, turn to Exercise 1 on page 38 for practice in identifying base grids. Analyze the blocks and ask yourself how many equal units are actually present across each design. Looking at quilt blocks in this way will give you a new perspective in analyzing the basic components of any pattern, and it's the first step toward drafting your own patterns!

 ## 2. Determine the Block Size

Once you have determined its base grid, you can decide what size you'd like the finished block to be. The simplest approach, whenever possible, is to work with a finished block size that's easily divisible by the number of equal units across the block. The measurement you give to each equal unit is called the *unit size* (the finished size of each unit, *without* seam allowances). The finished block size will equal the number of divisions across the block *times* this unit size. (Note that the finished block size refers to the size of the block *without* seam allowances.)

For example, let's work with a 9-patch block. If we assign a 2 1/2" measurement to each unit, the finished block size would be 3 x 2 1/2", or 7 1/2".

If you are making a sampler quilt, where you wish all of the blocks to be the same finished size, the unit sizes in each block will not always work out the same. For instance, if you were to make a 12" finished block with five equal divisions, each unit would be 12" ÷ 5, or 2 2/5".

If you were making an entire quilt of 5-patch blocks, you could choose to work with a block size that does divide evenly by the number 5, as shown.

However, there will be times when you will need to work with odd numbers such as 2 2/5". (Don't worry! We will cover this later.)

If you are working with different quilt blocks, it is helpful to keep a notebook to jot down notes and diagrams for each block. The following calculations

illustrate how you can make each of these quilt blocks in different sizes.

Double X

9-Patch

Base grid is a 9-patch.
2" per unit = 3 x 2" = 6" finished block.
2 1/2" per unit = 3 x 2 1/2" = 7 1/2" finished block.
4" per unit = 3 x 4" = 12" finished block.

Whirligig

Base grid is a 4-patch.
2" per unit = 4 x 2" = 8" finished block.
2 1/2" per unit = 4 x 2 1/2" = 10" finished block.
3" per unit = 4 x 3" = 12" finished block.

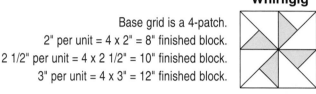

4-Patch

Wrench

Base grid is a 5-patch.
2" per unit = 5 x 2" = 10" finished block.
2 1/2" per unit = 5 x 2 1/2" = 12 1/2" finished block.
3" per unit = 5 x 3" = 15" finished block.

5-Patch

Bear's Paw

Base grid is a 7-patch.
1" per unit = 7 x 1" = 7" finished block.
1 1/2" per unit = 7 x 1 1/2" = 10 1/2" finished block.
2" per unit = 7 x 2" = 14" finished block.

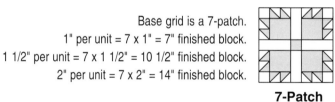

7-Patch

Now it's your turn. Look at the quilt blocks in Exercise 2 on page 39 and identify the number of equal units in the base grid. Find the unit size for a 12" finished block, and then assign a 1 1/2", 2" and a 2 1/2" measurement to each unit and determine the sizes of the finished blocks.

 ## 3. Identify the Pattern Pieces Needed

After you have selected a block pattern and determined its base grid and the number of equal units in it, using picture symbols for each of the pattern pieces will make it easy to recognize each shape needed. It is also easier to use picture symbols than to repeatedly write out "square," "rectangle" and "half-square triangle." The following diagrams illustrate some of the most commonly used shapes in patchwork blocks.

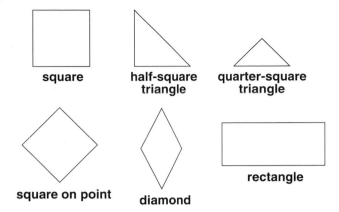

square   half-square triangle   quarter-square triangle

square on point   diamond   rectangle

For a *square*, determine the side of the square and write this measurement at the left of the symbol, as shown.

A *half-square triangle* is literally half of a square. For this kind of triangle, the side measurement is also placed at the left of the symbol, since this is the measurement you will need to know.

A *quarter-square triangle* is one-fourth of a square, as shown. The measurement should be noted under the base of the triangle because the base is the same length as one side of the square.

A *rectangle* requires two notations, since there are two different side measurements. Place the short measurement at the left of the symbol as shown and the long measurement below it.

For a *square on point*, write the diagonal measurement inside the symbol with small dashes point-

ing toward the four corners, as shown, since this is the known measurement.

The following is an example of a block with a square on point in the center. This is an 8" 4-patch block. Each unit is equal to 2". The distance from point to point across the center square (its diagonal) is equal to two of these units. Therefore, the diagonal measurement is 4". This is the measurement needed to draft this shape.

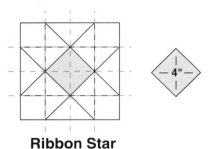

Ribbon Star

A *diamond* also has 4 equal sides. The measurement needed is the length of each side. This number should be placed at the left of the symbol, as shown.

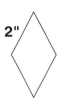

There is another group of commonly used shapes that are not as familiar by name as those above. I call these "etcetera" shapes. This category includes any shapes not previously discussed—parallelograms, trapezoids, etc. Draw picture symbols of these shapes and label all known measurements, as shown.

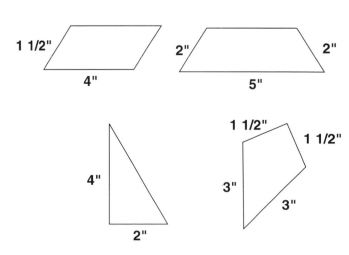

4. Determine the Finished Size of the Pattern Pieces

Now, let's analyze a specific block and determine the finished sizes of the pattern pieces required. The Shoo-Fly is a 9-patch. Two templates are needed to construct this block—a square and a half-square triangle.

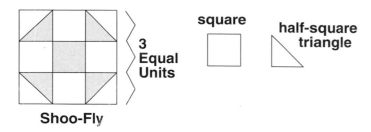

Shoo-Fly

To make a 3" Shoo-Fly block, the size of each equal unit would be 1" and the pattern notations would be as follows.

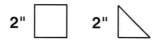

To make a 6" Shoo-Fly block, the equal units would be 2" and the pattern pieces would be as follows.

A 12" version would have an equal unit size of 4" and the pattern pieces would be as follows.

Using picture symbols is a great way to keep track of all the information you need to make templates. Here are more examples annotating base grids, equal units and shapes in a variety of quilt blocks.

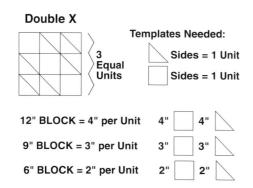

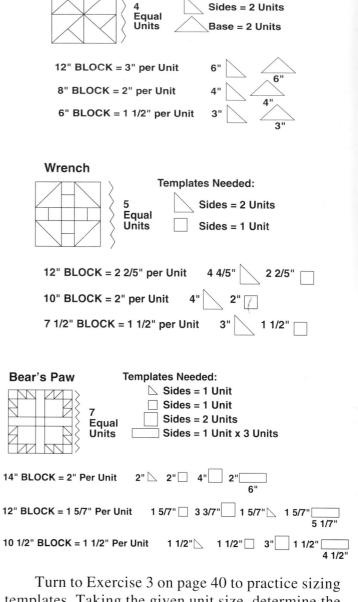

Turn to Exercise 3 on page 40 to practice sizing templates. Taking the given unit size, determine the correct size for each pattern piece.

Now you are ready to test what you've learned about drafting so far by completing Exercise 4 on page 41.

Occasionally, it is impossible to know the exact dimensions of an "etcetera" pattern piece. By knowing how many equal units of the block each shape fills, however, you can often draft the template correctly by measuring over, up or down from established lines in the pattern.

The Kentucky Chain is just such a block. It is a 4-patch with eight equal units in its base grid. In this example, the finished block size is 12". That means that each equal unit measures 1 1/2". The following diagrams illustrate how many equal units each shape fills. Three templates are needed to construct this block. The first template is a quarter-square triangle. Its baseline occupies 2 of the equal units of the base grid. This means that the base of this triangle is 3" long. The second template is an "etcetera" shape which is shown with a surrounding square indicated by broken lines. This square occupies 4 equal units, and the measurements of both the square and the template are noted. The third template is another "etcetera" shape, occupying 2 equal units. It is shown with the surrounding square indicated by broken lines, along with the necessary measurements for drafting this template.

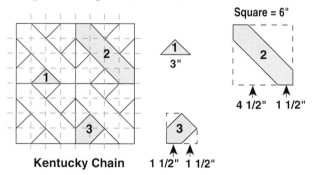

Kentucky Chain

5. Create the Templates
Drafting Pattern Pieces

After you have analyzed a quilt block and determined the necessary pattern pieces and their sizes, you are ready to begin drafting. Start by drawing the finished size of each pattern piece on graph paper. Whenever possible, use the darker grid lines on the graph paper.

Squares and *rectangles* are easy to draft—just follow the lines of the graph paper and draw the size you need, as shown.

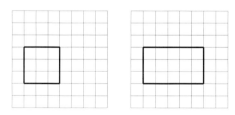

In a *half-square triangle,* the perpendicular sides are of equal length. Draw the perpendicular sides, then draw the diagonal line on the third side by connecting the endpoints, as shown.

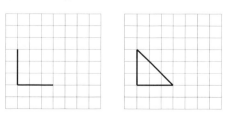

In a *quarter-square triangle,* the baseline is always equal to one side of the square. First, draw the baseline on graph paper. Then mark the midpoint of the baseline. To find the top point of the triangle, measure up from the midpoint the same distance as from the midpoint to the end of the baseline. Mark this point and connect it to each end of the baseline, as shown, to complete the triangle.

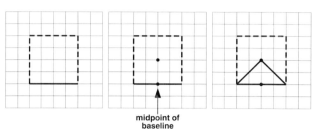

midpoint of baseline

To draft a *square on point,* you need to know the size of the outer *straight* square that surrounds the square on point. This measurement is the same as the *diagonal* measurement of the square on point. Draw a square this size and mark the midpoint on each side of the outer square. Connect these midpoints to complete the square on point. Place the diagonal measurement inside the square on point, as shown.

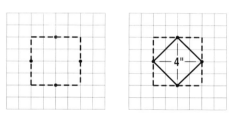

A *45° diamond* has four equal sides. Opposite angles are equal, as well. On a piece of graph paper, draw a line the length of one side. Lay a ruler at one end of this line, across the squares on the graph paper, at a 45° angle. Draw a second line that is longer than the first. Follow the same steps at the other end of the first line. With a compass or ruler, measure along both of these lines and place marks on each line at a distance that is equal to the first line. Connect these points to create the diamond.

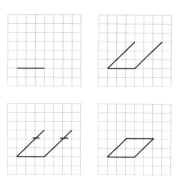

An *"etcetera"* shape can be drafted in the same manner as a square on point, by starting with measurements you know about the surrounding shape, marking key points with dots and connecting these dots.

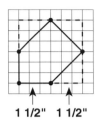 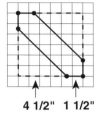

1 1/2"   1 1/2"   4 1/2"   1 1/2"

Adding Seam Allowances

Seam allowances are added after drawing the finished-size pattern piece. (Seam allowances are not marked for hand piecing.) If your graph paper has 4 or 8 squares per inch, the grid lines on the paper can be followed when adding seam allowances to straight pattern lines. Add these seam allowances first, as shown.

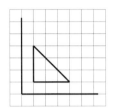

If the number of squares on the paper is not 4 or 8 per inch, or if the seam allowances do not fall on grid lines, use a ruler to add seam allowances. First, lay the ruler over the pattern piece, so that the 1/4" ruler line exactly matches one of the sewing lines on the pattern piece. Then back the ruler up just enough to allow for the width of the pencil line, as shown.

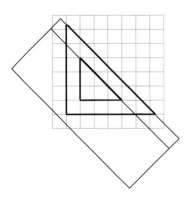

It is a good idea to use the same side of the same ruler each time you draft a pattern. To check the accuracy of your lines, place the middle of your ruler over the pattern piece. Make sure that the 1/4" grid lines on the ruler line up with the sewing line. If they do not match exactly, adjust the ruler and draw the correct line.

Trimming Points

You may wish to trim the long points ("dog ears") on triangles or diamond-shaped pattern pieces. This will make it easier to align pieces for sewing. On the two equal sides of a triangle, measure 1/4" beyond the endpoints, mark and trim, as shown. This creates a symmetrical template with cut edges that mirror each other.

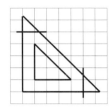 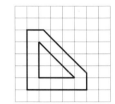

To trim the points of a diamond-shaped pattern piece, imagine a line running from tip to tip. Trim the tip perpendicular to this line, 1/4" beyond the point of the finished-size diamond, as shown.

Differently shaped pattern pieces should be considered individually and trimmed to 1/4" from the sewing line, as necessary.

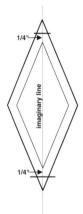

Drafting Odd-size Pattern Pieces

To draft a pattern that has equal units of an uneven measurement, a special size graph paper can be used. For example, a 12" block that has 5 equal units across and down the base grid will measure 2 2/5" per equal unit. Standard 1/4" graph paper will not work, but graph paper with 5 squares per inch makes it easy to draft such a pattern.

If the block you want to draft has equal units that do not fit your graph paper, follow these steps to draft the block on unlined paper. The example block is a 6" 7-patch block.

First, divide the block into 7 equal divisions:

1. Draw a square that is the size of the finished block (6").

2. Determine the number of equal units in the block (7).

3. Find a measurement *larger than the block size* that is divisible by the number of equal units. In this case, that measurement would be 7".

4. Now divide 7" by the number of equal units across and down the block. This gives you the intervals at which to mark division points along the ruler (1" intervals).

5. Position the 0" mark of the ruler at the lower left corner of the drawn block. Then place the 7" mark on the ruler so that it lies directly on the line at the right side of the block, as shown.

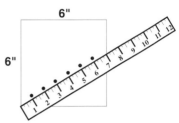

6. Mark a small dot at 1" intervals along the ruler, as shown.

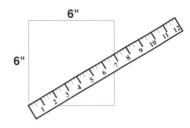

7. Draw lines through each of these division points, making sure that they are perpendicular to the bottom edge of the square, as shown.

8. Turn the block and repeat the process in the opposite direction. This will create a grid of seven equal units across and down the block.

Now that you have drafted a 6" square into a 7-patch, let's draw a Bear's Paw block on top of the grid.

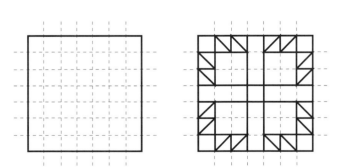

Using the Decimal System

Another option is to work with graph paper that has 10 squares per inch and use the decimal system. For example, if you wanted to draft a 12" block with seven equal units, you could divide 12" by 7 to get a

unit measurement of 1 5/7" *or* use the decimal system to arrive at a unit measurement of 1.7". The difference between a 1 5/7" triangle and a 1.7" triangle is minuscule, as shown by these triangles.

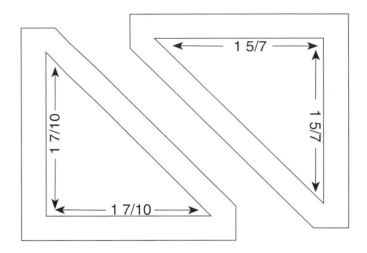

Making Templates

Cut out the graph paper pattern piece approximately 1/4" beyond the cutting line. Apply a layer of glue stick around the outer edges on the right side of the pattern piece. (On large pieces, mark an X or Z across the center of the piece with the glue stick to make the plastic adhere better to the paper.) Place the template plastic on top of the graph paper and smooth the two together firmly. Check to be sure that there is no rippling or bubbling between the layers. Glue the wrong side of a piece of sandpaper to the wrong side of the graph paper, creating a template "sandwich." Cut the template out on the cutting lines. (For hand piecing, cut the template out on the sewing lines.) This kind of template is permanent and very sturdy because of the glued-together layers. The sandpaper will "grab" the fabric, which helps prevent slipping.

Label each template with its size, grainline and the name of the block pattern. When I plan to use a template for more than one pattern, I call it a "master template." Master templates do not need to be labeled with the name of a particular pattern. Necessary information such as template size and grainlines can be marked on the master template or written on a Post-It™ note that can be placed temporarily on the template. Other helpful information, such as how many pieces to cut and in which colors for a particular pattern can also be marked on a Post-It note and attached to the template. This is easy to remove after your project is finished.

Storing Templates

Store templates in a commonsense manner so that they are easily accessible. Find the storage system you like best—one that is convenient and that you will use consistently.

One method is to use clear plastic zippered pouches in which templates can be easily seen. These handy pouches can be stored in a three-ring notebook, drawer or bookcase.

Another way to store templates is to glue them on a piece of paper. This paper can be slipped into a top-loading page protector. Page protectors are transparent and can also be kept in a three-ring notebook for easy accessibility.

Small, sturdy cardboard or plastic boxes are also good for storing templates. Each box could be labeled with the shapes and sizes of the templates it holds.

Master Templates

The following master templates are commonly used in quilt blocks. If you make these master templates in the sizes given, you may want to experiment with many different block patterns!

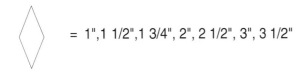

= 1", 1 1/2", 1 3/4", 2", 2 1/2", 3", 3 1/2", 4", 4 1/2", 5", 5 1/2", 6"

= 1", 1 1/2", 1 3/4", 2", 2 1/2", 3", 3 1/2", 4", 4 1/2", 5", 5 1/2", 6"

= 2", 2 1/2", 3", 3 1/2", 4", 4 1/2", 5", 5 1/2", 6"

= 1", 1 1/2", 1 3/4", 2", 2 1/2", 3", 3 1/2"

NOTE: *Patterns for these master templates are provided on page 62. Do not trace them! They are provided for you to compare with your templates to ensure that you are making them correctly before cutting your fabric.*

Grainline

Just what is *grain* and what does it mean to quilters? To understand what grain is we need to understand a bit about how cotton fabric is created. Cotton fabric is woven, meaning the fibers weave over and under one another to create the tightly packed web which we call fabric.

Selvages are the tightly finished edges which run the length of the fabric. The fabric is held on the machines by the selvages during the dyeing and printing processes. Selvages do not ravel. They should never be used in your quilts, but should be removed during the cutting process.

The lengthwise fibers which run parallel to the selvages are the *straight* grain. The width-wise fibers which are perpendicular to the selvages are the *cross* grain. At a 45° angle to the straight and cross grains runs the *bias* grain. If you take your fabric and fold it so that the *straight* and *cross* grains match up, the fold edge is the *bias*. There is virtually no stretch to the *straight* grain of a fabric. There is a slight amount of stretch to the *cross* grain. *Bias* grain, on the other hand, has a considerable amount of stretchiness.

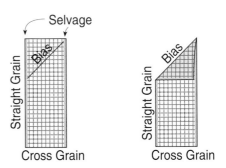

As quilters we use the phrase "straight grain" to refer to either the true straight *or* the cross grain. The grainline arrow on our templates can either be aligned with the straight or the cross grain of the fabric. We must avoid, however, aligning the bias grain where it can adversely affect the stability of the block and/or quilt.

When you are using a commercial pattern, the grainline arrows are usually already indicated on the pattern pieces. But what about when you are drafting the block yourself? How do you know which edges of which pattern pieces should be straight grain and which can be on the bias?

The first thing to consider is the block's outside edges. It is best to have straight grain all around the outside of the block. Blocks constructed this way are less likely to stretch and distort, thus preventing problems in assembling your quilt.

Using the Sawtooth Star block as an example, if the side triangles were cut with the two short edges on the straight grain, the bias would be positioned on the outside edges of the block. This block would likely stretch along these edges making the block untrue. This triangle should be cut with its long edge on the straight grain.

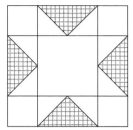 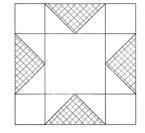

Correct Grain Placement   Incorrect Grain Placement

Some inner pieces are important to consider, too. Consider how a block is to be assembled. Pieces are often sewn into smaller units first, then these units are assembled into the finished block. Blocks may have many units, and even subunits, that are constructed first. Decide how the block breaks down into units. By constructing the most stable units, we make the most stable blocks. Avoid set-in piecing whenever possible.

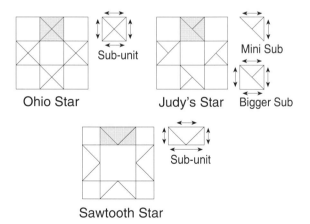

Ohio Star   Judy's Star   Bigger Sub

Sub-unit   Mini Sub

Sawtooth Star   Sub-unit

Now assign straight grain to the outside edges of the block units. It is important to note here that you will not always be able to sew bias to straight grain and still have straight grain around the outside edges of your block. While this would be ideal, trying to analyze a block to allow for this kind of construction could drive you crazy. Do not be overly concerned about sewing bias grain to bias. While sewing two bias edges together is more difficult and you must take care not to stretch the seam as you sew, with experience you will learn to take the necessary care and precaution when dealing with pieces that may distort.

Like everything in quilting, there are exceptions to these guidelines. For example, if you are using a striped fabric and you want that stripe to create a definite pattern in the block, you will have to ignore grain. Just be aware of where the grain is, both on the individual units as well as the finished block and be careful.

In other places, grain must be a primary consideration. One of the most important places to be stalwart about grainline is in the setting triangles that finish the outer edges of a quilt with diagonally set blocks. A quilt with bias along these edges will almost never hang straight. The weight of the quilt pulls along the bias grain of these edges causing it to sag and ripple. When using templates to cut setting triangles there is usually little confusion about how to position them for the desired grainline. More often, the confusion comes in when quilters opt to cut those triangles without templates. (Please refer to the section on "Setting Triangles" in Chapter 4, page 45.)

There is also some controversy over the placement of grainline in border strips. Some quilters believe that you must cut border strips on the straight grain, because there is less give and stretch. I prefer to cut my strips selvage to selvage (on the cross grain) and have not found the minor stretch of the cross grain to pose a problem. The decision to cut border strips on the straight or cross grain is entirely up to you. ◢

CHAPTER II

Drafting Eight-Pointed Stars

Simple Eight-Pointed Stars

Now let's look at another category of blocks known as eight-pointed stars. These blocks are based on the division of a circle into eight equal segments and are composed of 45° diamonds.

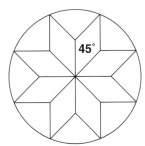

LeMoyne Star

The simplest eight-pointed star block is the LeMoyne Star. Unlike "grid" stars, the sides of these blocks cannot be equally divided. The distance from point to point, however, *is* equal.

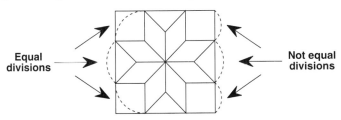

Three pieces are required for this star block: a square (four equal sides), a 45° diamond (also four equal sides) and a half-square triangle (equal to half the size of the corner square). If we know the size of the corner square, we can determine the size of the diamond and the half-square triangle.

If you were working with a grid star and wanted to know the measurement of the corner square, you would decide on the block size and simply add up the number of equal divisions along the side and divide that number into the size of the block.

Example: 12" Variable Star (4-Patch)

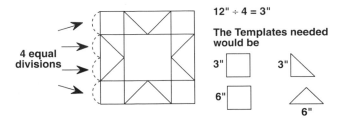

The LeMoyne Star is not a grid star, yet the divisions along the sides do have a relationship with one another. That relationship is based on a simplification of the Pythagorean Theorem as applied to finding the diagonal of a square (or the long side of a half-square triangle). This may sound complicated, but it's not!

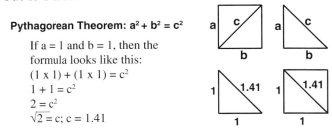

Pythagorean Theorem: $a^2 + b^2 = c^2$

If $a = 1$ and $b = 1$, then the formula looks like this:
$(1 \times 1) + (1 \times 1) = c^2$
$1 + 1 = c^2$
$2 = c^2$
$\sqrt{2} = c; c = 1.41$

This simplification proves that the diagonal of a square is always 1.41 times longer than the side (1.41 being the square root of 2). Always—no exceptions!

So what has this to do with eight-pointed stars? Look at the LeMoyne Star again with that magic number, 1.41, in mind.

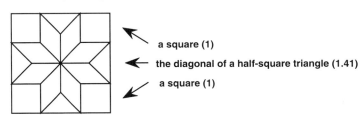

a square (1)

the diagonal of a half-square triangle (1.41)

a square (1)

This makes the sum of the parts along the side:

1 + 1.41 + 1 = 3.41

Take the size of the block you wish to make and divide by the sum of the parts:

Example: 12" ÷ 3.41 = 3.5"

Therefore, the corner square is 3 1/2". Because the square fits exactly to one side of the diamond, the sides of the diamond are also 3 1/2", and the half-square triangle is 3 1/2" on the short sides.

It doesn't matter what size LeMoyne Star block you want to make. The sum of the parts is always the same. It's helpful to use a hand-held calculator rather than do long division. The calculator will, of course, always give you a decimal response. The decimal must be converted to a fraction for use with graph paper.

See the Decimal Equivalent Chart on page 69 to assist you in converting a decimal to a workable fraction. Not all decimals have fractional equivalents that you can work with. You will sometimes run into numbers that need to be adjusted slightly to be more easily converted into workable fractions. It is important to be very careful when doing this. We tend to think that the amount we are adding to or subtracting from the decimal is so minute that it "can't matter," when in truth it can.

Example: 8" LeMoyne Star block

8" ÷ 3.41 = 2.34"

If you drop the 4 and use 2 3/10" (2.3") as your fraction, then the resulting block will be:

2.3 x 3.41 = 7.843"

This is smaller than the 8" block by almost 1/5" (0.2").

On the other hand, if you were to use 2 1/3 as your fraction, the block would be 2.33" x 3.41 = 7.945". Now you are less than 5/100 of an inch smaller, significantly less than the 1/5" above.

You should always be aware of the consequences when adjusting a decimal. If you are repeating one block pattern throughout your quilt, the blocks will all measure the same size and fit together, so the fraction you choose to work with is less important. If you are using different block patterns in one quilt, as in a sampler, then you usually choose a block size that is appropriate to all the blocks. It is very important to be careful choosing your fractions in this case.

Sometimes the decision on which fraction to use will be based on which graph paper you use. But remember, if the graph paper you select is anything

other than 4 or 8 to the inch, you must add all seam allowances with a ruler. None can be added with the lines on the graph paper.

If the decimal will not convert to a workable fraction, round it off to the nearest tenth of an inch and use 10-to-the-inch graph paper.

Example: 10" block

10" ÷ 3.41 = 2.93

Templates required:

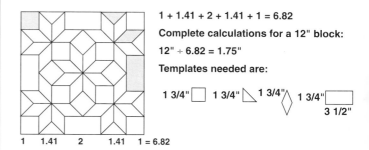

Using the calculator and working with decimals will become easier as you begin to understand how to use the 1 and 1.41 values. Just as you added those values together for the simple eight-pointed star and came up with 3.41, you will analyze other blocks and use those values to determine the actual templates needed.

Snow Crystal

Study the outside edge of the block. If the side of the corner square is 1, the long side of the rectangle is 1 + 1 = 2, and the long side of the triangle is equal to 1.41, then the sum of the parts along the edge is:

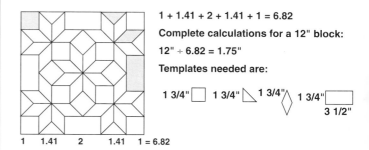

1 + 1.41 + 2 + 1.41 + 1 = 6.82

Complete calculations for a 12" block:

12" ÷ 6.82 = 1.75"

Templates needed are:

1 3/4" 1 3/4" 1 3/4" 1 3/4" 3 1/2"

Carpenter's Wheel

Along the edge of this block are four squares (or 1 values) and two triangle bases (or 1.41 values). The sum of the parts along the edge is:

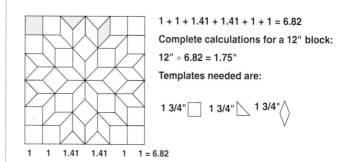

1 + 1 + 1.41 + 1.41 + 1 + 1 = 6.82

Complete calculations for a 12" block:

12" ÷ 6.82 = 1.75"

Templates needed are:

1 3/4" 1 3/4" 1 3/4"

Virginia Star

This block is related to the Lone Star. It is based on subdividing the large diamond of the eight-pointed star into equal, smaller diamonds. Begin with the size of the finished block and find the sum of the parts to determine how big the corner square and side triangles will be. How many equal small diamonds fit along the edge of the corner square? You can have as many rows of small diamonds as you want. In this example there are 3.

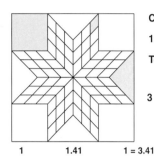

Complete calculations for a 12" block:

12" ÷ 3.41 = 3.5" ÷ 3 = 1.166 = 1 1/6"

Templates needed are:

3 1/2" □   3 1/2" ◺   1 1/6" ◇

1   1.41   1 = 3.41

Blazing Star

This one starts out like the Virginia Star, but how do we find the other templates? We divide by 2 because in this example 2 small diamonds fit along the edge of the corner square.

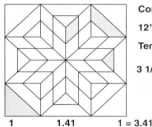

Complete calculations for a 12" block:

12" ÷ 3.41 = 3.5" ÷ 2 = 1 3/4"

Templates needed are:

1   1.41   1 = 3.41

Octagonal Stars

The relationship that exists on the sides of an equal-sided octagon is the same as that between the points of the eight-pointed star.

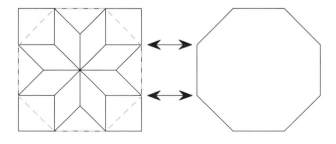

The relationship of this octagon placed inside a square is the same as that of an eight-pointed star inside a square.

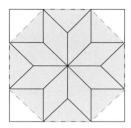

Rolling Star

In this block, the octagon is formed by diamonds laid on their sides. The length of the two sides of the diamonds on the outer edge is equal to the 1.41 value which would fit between star points on a regular eight-pointed star. Therefore, the calculations would be based on a total of 3.41 along the edge of the block:

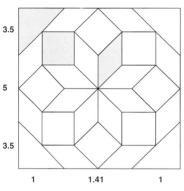

Begin the calculations with 12" ÷ 3.41 = 3.5", which tells you the size of the corner triangle.

That number times 1.41 will give you the distance between the corner triangles: 3.5" x 1.41 = 5". (Or, 12" - (2 x 3.5") = 5")

This number when divided by 2 will tell you the length of one of the diamonds, which in turn tells you the size of the square.

Complete calculations for a 12" block:

12" ÷ 3.41 = 3.5" x 1.41 = 4.96" ÷ 2 = 2.5"

Templates needed are:

3 1/2" □   2 1/2" ◺   2 1/2" ◇

Star of the Magi

This graceful block may take a little more thinking time, but the result is worth the investment. Study the block.

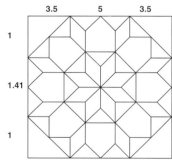

Note the location of the diamonds, in each "corner" of the octagon. Between the points of the diamonds, all around the octagon, are half-square triangles. Just as with Rolling Star, begin your calculations with the block size divided by 3.41.

Example: 12" block - 12" ÷ 3.41 = 3.5"

The size of the four corner triangles is 3 1/2" on the short sides. This answer multiplied by 1.41 tells us the distance between the diamond points, which must be divided by two to determine the long base of the half-square triangles. To find the side length of those triangles, that answer is divided by 1.41.

From the beginning the calculations are:

$$12" \div 3.41 = 3.5" \qquad 4.96" \div 2 = 2.5"$$
$$3.5" \times 1.41 = 4.96" \qquad 2.5" \div 1.41 = 1.75"$$

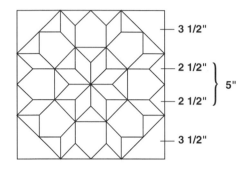

We now know the size of the ◺ , ◊ , and four sides of the ⌂.

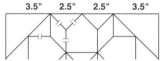

Now you must determine the base of ⌂. There are several ways to arrive at this measurement. Half the length of the base of the half-square triangle is 1 1/4". The length of the base of ⌂ is twice this measurement: 1 1/4" x 2 = 2 1/2". Therefore, the base of ⌂ is 2 1/2".

You may find it easier to visualize that the "roof" of this piece is the same as the half-square triangle for which we already know the length of the base (2 1/2"). And the length of the base of ⌂ is equal to that length = 2 1/2".

If the base of ⌂ is 2 1/2", then the side of the triangle with the 2 1/2" base is

2.5" ÷ 1.41 = 1.75"

Therefore, the ◺ and the ◊ must also be 1 3/4".

Templates needed for Star of the Magi are

1 3/4"◊ 1 3/4"◺ 3 1/2"◺ 1 3/4"⌂1 3/4" (2 1/2") (1 3/4")

Feathered Stars

Not all Feathered Stars are based on the eight-pointed star division. Some are grid stars. Let's draft an eight-pointed variation, a 15" block with 3" feathers flanking the points of the star. Study the outer edge of the block. Add the sum of the values which fit along the edge. (For your ease and convenience I have numbered and labeled the various templates required.)

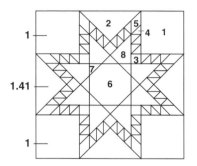

15" ÷ 3.41 = 4.39" (4 4/10", which reduces to 4 2/5").

Therefore, the actual size of the square in the corner (template 1) is 4 2/5".

The base (short side) of the triangle (template 2) is also 4 2/5".

To find the size of the feathers, add the 1 and 1.41 values which fit along the side of the corner square. In the example, there are three triangles (or 1 values) and one diamond (or (1) 1.41 value). (The side of the diamond is equal to the long side of the half-square triangle, which is 1.41 times longer than its side.)

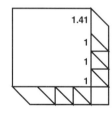

Example: 1 + 1 + 1 + 1.41 = 4.41

15" ÷ 3.41 = 4.39" ÷ 4.41 = .99" (1").

Hence the "feather" triangle (template 4) is a 1" ◺ and the square (template 3) is a 1" ☐.

To find the size of the diamond at the star tip, multiply the size of the feather (template 4) by 1.41.

.99" x 1.41 = 1.4" (1 4/10" = 1 2/5") - template 5 = 1 2/5"

To find the size of the octagon in the center, start with the size of the block and subtract the corner square and the width of the row of feathers *twice*. You will be left with the size of the square in the middle of the block, into which the octagon fits:

15" - 4.39 = 10.61" - 4.39 = 6.22" - .99 = 5.23" - .99 = 4.24"
(template 1)   (1)   (template 4)   (4)   (4 1/4")

Determined: The octagon in the center is 4 1/4" across.

Template 6 = 4 1/4" ⬡.

This octagon followed the same divisions as the eight-pointed star. To determine the size of the corner triangles, take the size of the square, which we just found, and divide by 3.41:

4.24" ÷ 3.41 = 1.24" (1 1/4"). Determined: Template 7 = 1 1/4"

The short sides of the triangle exactly match the short edges of the "kite" shape. Therefore, the short side of the kite is 1 1/4". The long side of the kite is equal to the sum of three feathers. Since each feather has been determined to be 1", the long side of the kite must be 3".

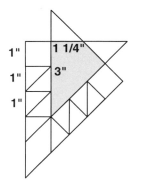

Templates needed for this 15" Feathered Star are

(1) 4 2/5" □   (2) 4 2/5" ◺   (3) 1" □   (4) 1" ◺

(5) 1 2/5" ◇   (6) 4 1/4" ○   (7) 1 1/4" ◺   (8) 3" ◿ 1 1/4"

To draft any other size Feathered Star, begin by assigning the block size and establishing how many feathers there will be per point. Then follow the above procedure to determine the new pattern piece sizes.

Now, turn to Exercise 5 on page 42 to practice drafting Eight-Pointed Stars. ◪

Drafting Fans and Other Circular Blocks

When most quilters think of fan blocks, Grandmother's Fan comes to mind and little else. But there are so many possibilities for this quarter-circle design unit! And if you multiply it by four, you have a full circle, opening doors to drafting patterns like Mariner's Compass, Dresden Plate and Sunburst. By working with fan designs, you will realize that you don't have to draft an entire circle. Everything you need for a circular pattern is right there, in that quarter-circle.

In this chapter, you'll learn how to make any size fan block, with any number of blades and any "extras" you desire. You will control all aspects of the pattern—the number of blades, shape of the top edge, blade design and final size!

The basic block consists of three parts: background (A), blades (B) and handle (C).

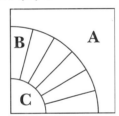

The blades may be simple pie-shaped wedges, or they may be complex subdivided units. Where they touch the background, the top edges of the blades may be a continuous, gentle curve, or they may be scalloped or pointed. For our purposes, fans will be broken down into four separate categories and defined as follows:

1) *Grandmother's Fans*
• Smooth, continuous, curved outer edge.
• Usually pieced into the background square.
• May have any number of blades.
• Simple or complex blade structure.

2) *Pointed-top Fans*
• Pieced fans which may be pieced into background or appliquéd to background square.
• Simple or complex blade structure.

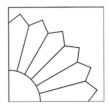

3) *Scalloped-top Fans*
• Always appliquéd to base square.
• Arcs may be very high, very low or in between.

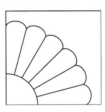

4) *Faceted Fans*
• Structurally resemble Mariner's Compasses, Sunbursts, etc.

All fans will be pieced, fitting into the corner of a square, at a 90° angle. Begin by deciding how many blades you desire for your fan block. Then, divide 90° by the number of blades desired to find the measurement of the blade angle.

Example:
    3 fan blades: 90° ÷ 3 = 30° each
    4 fan blades: 90° ÷ 4 = 22.5° each
    5 fan blades: 90° ÷ 5 = 18° each
    6 fan blades: 90° ÷ 6 = 15° each
    7 fan blades: 90° ÷ 7 = 12.85° each
    8 fan blades: 90° ÷ 8 = 11.25° each
    9 fan blades: 90° ÷ 9 = 10° each
    10 fan blades: 90° ÷ 10 = 9° each

Grandmother's Fans

Using removable tape, position graph paper on a cutting mat, a piece of foam core or cardboard. Draw a square on your graph paper the exact size you want the *finished* fan block to be.

Place the point of the compass exactly in one corner of the square (Point A). Draw an arc to establish the handle and another arc to establish the outer edge of the fan.

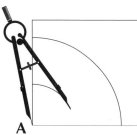

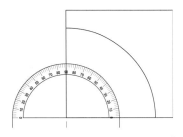

Position the protractor so that the 90° angle is on the north/south line and the baseline markers are at the inside corner.

With a sharp pencil, mark off every X° on the handle arc. (X is dependent upon the number of blades desired.) Example: 6 divisions = 15°; mark at 15°, 30°, 45°, 60°, 75°.

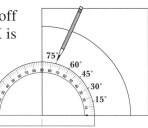

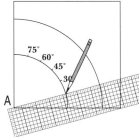

Remove the protractor. Lay a ruler from one mark to Point A. Draw a straight line through the mark, from the outer arc to the handle arc. Repeat for each mark.

Exercise:

Practice drafting a 6" Grandmother's Fan block (handle arc: 1 3/4" from Point A; outer arc: 5 1/2" from Point A). Try five blades, then four or even ten. Come up with some of your own!

Pointed-top Fans

These fans can be entirely pieced, or they may incorporate hand appliqué to attach the pieced fan to a background block.

Directional Blade Fan

The blades in this type of fan block are directional. It is important when cutting out the blade pieces that all the fabric be positioned right side up or you will not be able to use all the blades in the same fan block.

To begin drafting, draw a square on graph paper the exact size you want the finished fan block to be. Using a compass, draw an arc for the handle and one to mark the outer edge of the blades. Use a protractor to measure, mark, and divide the fan into the desired number of blades. Lightly mark a third "reference" arc inside the outer arc. Draw a line from the outer arc to the reference arc across the width of the fan blade as shown.

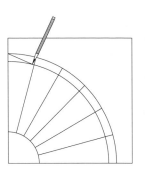

The farther apart the reference arc is from the outside arc, the steeper the angle of the blade will be.

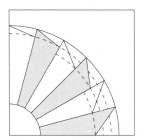

Symmetrical Blade Fan

Other pointed-top fan blocks have symmetrical fan blades. Begin drafting the same as above: draw a square, mark three arcs and divide into equal blade units with a protractor.

There are two ways to mark the points at the top of the blades. The first is simply to draw an "x" inside each blade between the outer arc and the reference arc as shown.

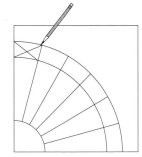

Another way to mark the points is to find the center point of each blade unit with your protractor. Then, draw lines from the reference arc to this center point as shown.

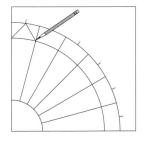

Again, the further apart the reference arc and the outer arc, the more pointed the fan block will be.

You may wish to divide each blade unit into two halves and color each half with a different fabric. This will result in a three-dimensional fan block, like a real fan with folds.

Pyramid Fan

This fan is a series of concentric arcs which are divided into six 15° partitions. The divisions on the outer ring begin at the edge. The divisions on the next ring begin 7.5° in and are then measured every 15°, ending 7.5° from the adjacent edge.

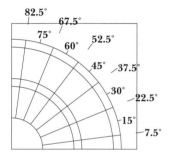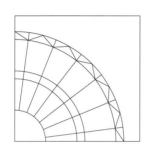

Scalloped-top Fans

On graph paper draw a square the size you want the finished fan block to be. Using a compass, draw the handle arc and an outer arc to serve as a placement line for the low point of the scallop.

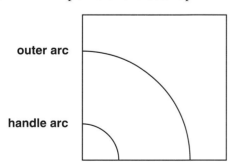

Next, draw a reference arc inside the outer arc.

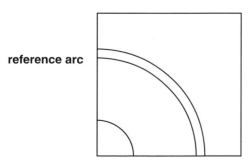

The closer the reference arc is to the outer arc the higher the scallop will be. Likewise, the further the reference arc is from the outer arc the flatter the scallop will be.

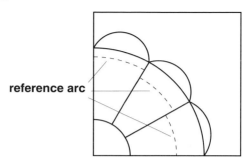

Use a protractor to measure, mark and divide the fan into the desired number of blades. Draw blade lines from the handle arc to the outer arc. Then, measure and mark the midpoints between blades on the reference arc.

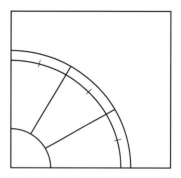

Position the compass point at one of the midpoints on the reference arc. Extend the compass pencil to the end of a blade where it hits the outer arc. Draw the scallop by rotating the compass pencil from the first blade line to the next blade line.

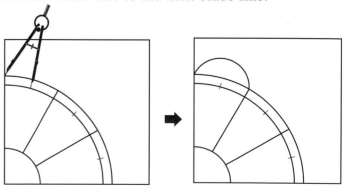

Consider splitting the fan blade and using two different fabrics. Strip piecing the two fabrics together before cutting the blade out can save time in piecing, as well as in the template-making stage, because fewer templates are required.

A Sunflower fan has pointed, scalloped blades. To draft this block, position the point of the compass where one fan blade intersects the outer arc, extend the pencil to the other side of the blade and rotate upwards. Repeat from the other side. The point of the blade occurs where the two arcs cross.

How about a combination scalloped- and pointed-top fan block?

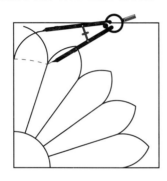

Put four scalloped-top fan blocks together to make a Dresden Plate block.

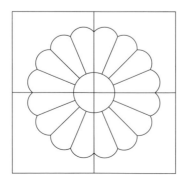

Make a complete Sunflower block with four Sunflower fans.

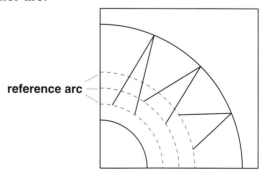

Faceted Fans

These blocks are not based on the typical bladed fan blocks but rather on the Sunburst and Mariner's Compass patterns. The similarity between these blocks and traditional fan blocks is that they are based on a quarter-circle, and it takes a compass and protractor to create each of them.

Liberty Fan

To draft the faceted Liberty Fan block, start with a square the size of the desired finished block. Draw an outer arc to serve as the outer perimeter of the fan design and an inner arc for the handle. Draw a third reference arc. The closer the inner arc is to the reference arc, the thinner the points will be. For wider points, the third arc should be 3/4" or more away from the inner arc.

Use the protractor to divide the outer arc into four equal sections, each marked at 22.5° intervals.

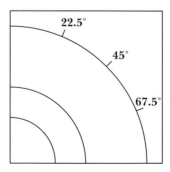

For the inner intervals, which are halfway between the divisions of the outer arc, measure over 11.25° on the reference arc, make a mark and then mark again every 22.5°.

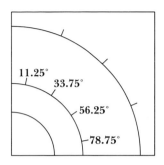

Lay your ruler from the point where the outer arc meets the left edge of the square to the first mark on the reference arc and draw a line.

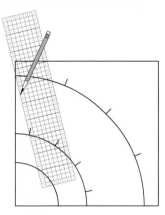

Now, connect the first mark on the reference arc to the first mark on your outer arc. Continue connecting marks to create a spoke-like effect as shown. (Doesn't this fan remind you of the Statue of Liberty's crown?)

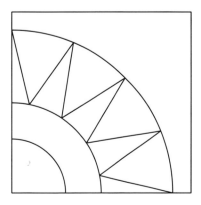

Compass Fan

This fan is drafted in the same way as the Liberty Fan. There are seven equal divisions on the outer arc, so marks are made along the outer arc every 12.85°. The inner reference arc is marked first at 6.425°, and

then every 12.85°. Once again, lines are drawn back and forth to create the "compass" points.

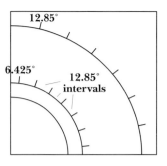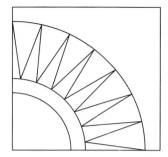

Making Fan Templates

After the fan pattern is drawn, you must decide what templates you need. For the simple Grandmother's Fan, there are three templates.

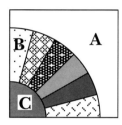

Tape the drawing on cardboard. Position template plastic on top of the drawing—be conservative with the plastic, but remember to leave space for seam allowances. Tape the plastic to the paper with the removable tape.

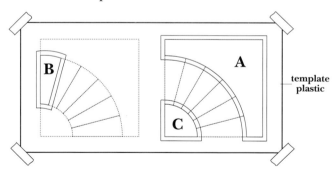

Trace each pattern piece carefully one at a time. Add seam allowances to each one. Mark straight edges with the ruler and curved edges with the compass. Position the compass at Point A, as before. For seam allowance on an outer curve, extend the compass pencil point 1/4" and draw the arc.

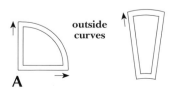

For seam allowance on inside curves, decrease the compass pencil position by 1/4" and draw the arc.

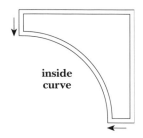

inside curve

Cut the template plastic carefully with paper cutting scissors.

A variety of fan blocks is shown on page 58 for more inspiration. Have fun. I design a lot more blocks than I actually construct. Don't be limited by these designs. Be adventurous! Designing can be half the fun, if you let it be, and you'll be amazed how easy it actually is.

Blade Makers

The most difficult part of drafting fan blocks is reading the protractor and measuring and marking accurately. If you are off by even 1° for a fan with 10 blades, that amounts to 10° by the time you are finished constructing the block. It's no wonder that fan blocks have a tendency to become distorted. At least with fans we can straighten the blocks up after-wards to make them square and flat. You don't have that luxury when making full-circle blocks such as Mariner's Compass and Dresden Plate!

The "blade makers" on pages 35-37 will ensure successful measuring. There are three different blade makers, each labelled with the number of divisions and how many blades are potentially possible. The blade maker eliminates the need for a protractor, and includes only the divisions that you need to be concerned with for the particular fan block you are drafting. If you are making a fan with five blades, you don't need to look at lines which would divide the block into six, seven or eight divisions.

Tape the blade maker to your work surface. (A rotary mat is great for this.) Tape a piece of heavy-weight tracing paper on top of the blade maker and trace the lines needed to construct the fan of choice. Several reference and construction arcs are provided with each blade maker, but you can add more if you wish. Always use a compass and ruler to draw or trace the necessary arcs and straight lines, for the most accurate templates.

Using the blade makers can save lots of time and increase accuracy. Remember, the blade makers can also be used to draft all those circular blocks—Mariner's Compass, Sunflower, Dresden Plate, etc. You need to draw only one-fourth of the block to draft the required templates. ◢

Blade Maker

for 3, 4, 6 and 12 blades

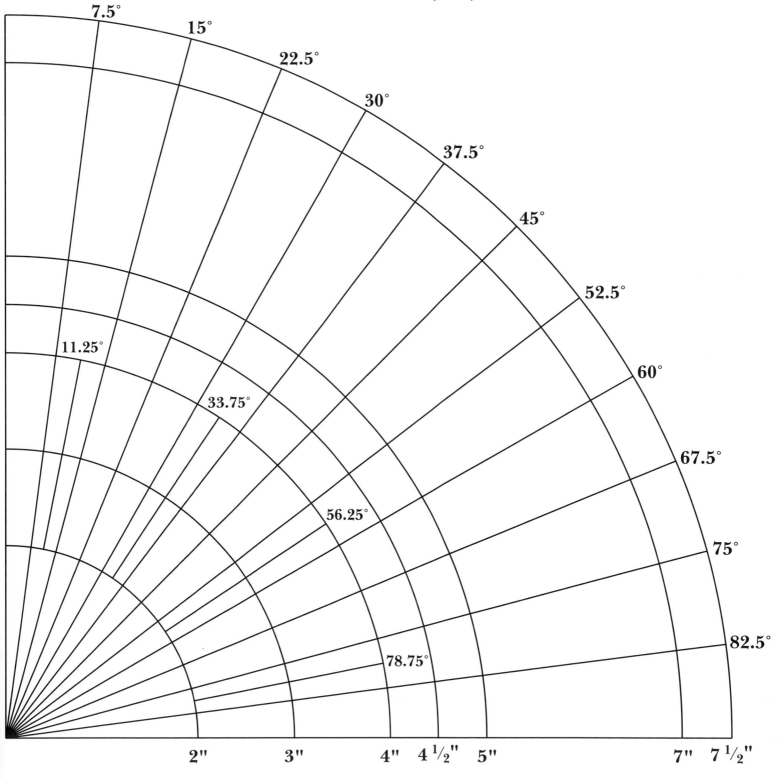

7.5°
15°
22.5°
30°
37.5°
45°
52.5°
60°
67.5°
75°
82.5°

11.25°
33.75°
56.25°
78.75°

2"   3"   4"   4 ½"   5"   7"   7 ½"

Blade Maker

for 5 and 10 blades

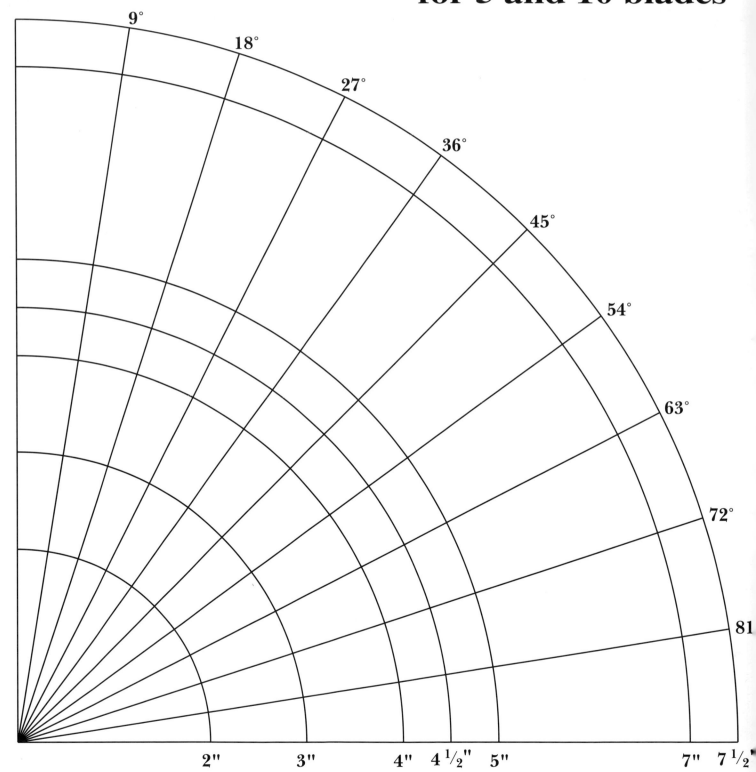

9° 18° 27° 36° 45° 54° 63° 72° 81°

2" 3" 4" 4 1/2" 5" 7" 7 1/2"

Blade Maker

for 7 and 14 blades

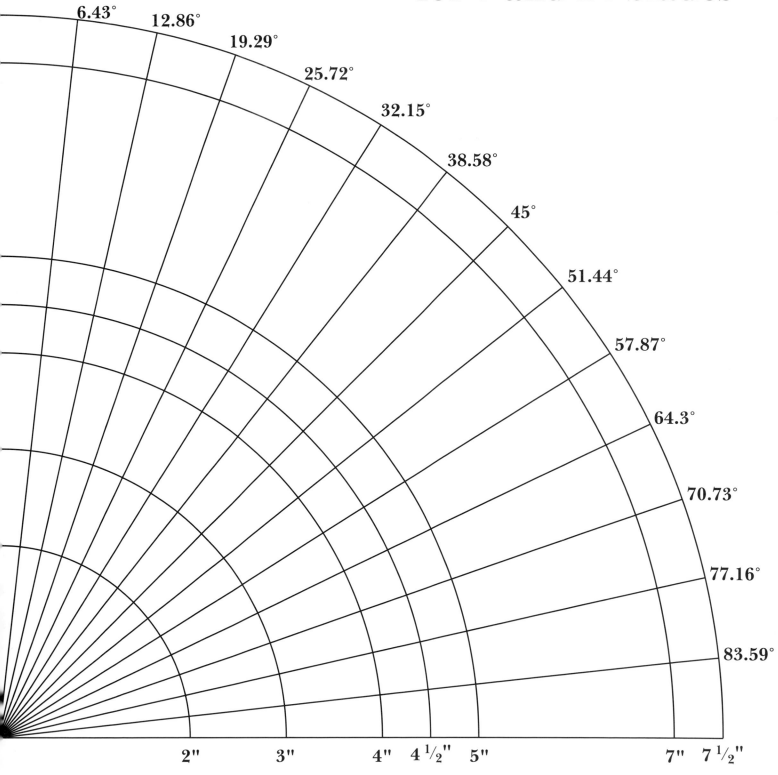

6.43° 12.86° 19.29° 25.72° 32.15° 38.58° 45° 51.44° 57.87° 64.3° 70.73° 77.16° 83.59°

2" 3" 4" 4 ½" 5" 7" 7 ½"

Exercise 1

Identifying Base Grids

Analyze the following quilt blocks to determine the base grid. How many equal divisions are there across and down each block? (Answers are given on page 59.)

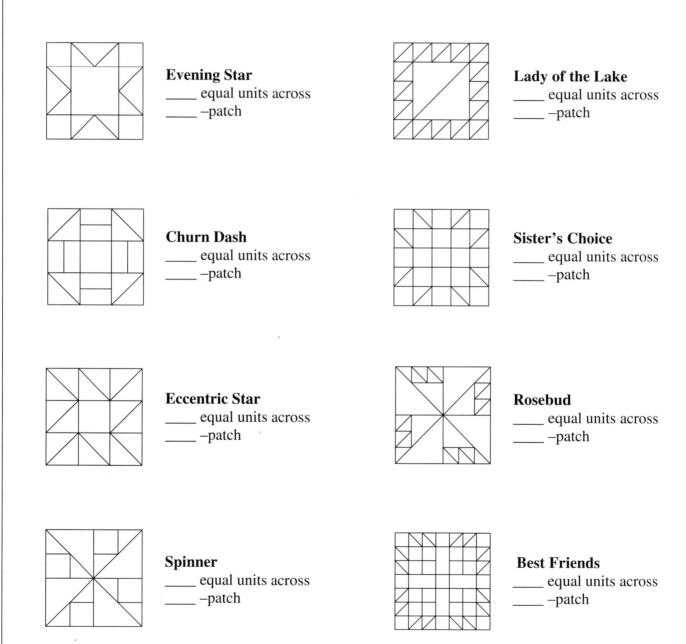

Evening Star
_____ equal units across
_____ –patch

Lady of the Lake
_____ equal units across
_____ –patch

Churn Dash
_____ equal units across
_____ –patch

Sister's Choice
_____ equal units across
_____ –patch

Eccentric Star
_____ equal units across
_____ –patch

Rosebud
_____ equal units across
_____ –patch

Spinner
_____ equal units across
_____ –patch

Best Friends
_____ equal units across
_____ –patch

Exercise 2

Drafting Blocks in Different Sizes

Identify the number of equal units in the base grid of each of the following blocks. Find the unit size for a 12" finished block. Then assign the given measurements to each unit and determine the sizes of the finished blocks. (Answers are given on page 59.)

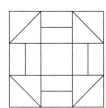

Evening Star
Base grid has ___equal units across.
Unit size for a 12" block:____
1 1/2" units = ____" block
2" units = _____" block
2 1/2" units = ____" block

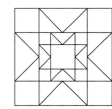

Star Within a Star
Base grid has ___ equal units across.
Unit size for a 12" block:____
1" units = ____" block
2" units = _____" block
2 1/2" units = ____" block

Churn Dash
Base grid has ___ equal units across.
Unit size for a 12" block:____
1 1/2" units = ____" block
2" units = _____" block
2 1/2" units = ____" block

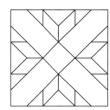

Swing in the Center
Base grid has ___ equal units across.
Unit size for a 12" block:____
1" units = ____" block
1 1/2" units = _____" block
3 1/2" units = ____" block

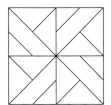

Wheels
Base grid has ___ equal units across.
Unit size for a 12" block:____
1" units = ____" block
2" units = _____" block
3 1/2" units = ____" block

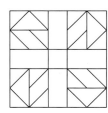

Jack-in-the-Box
Base grid has ___ equal units across.
Unit size for a 12" block:____
1 1/2" units = ____" block
2" units = _____" block
3" units = ____" block

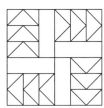

Boardwalk
Base grid has ___ equal units across.
Unit size for a 12" block:____
1 1/2" units = ____" block
2 1/2" units = ____" block
3" units = _____" block

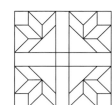

Hands Together
Base grid has ___ equal units across.
Unit size for a 12" block:____
1 1/2" units = ____" block
2" units = _____" block
2 1/2" units = ____" block

Exercise 3

Template Sizing

The following patchwork blocks are shown with base grid lines and picture symbols for the necessary pattern pieces. With the given unit size, find the correct measurements for each template. (Answers are given on page 60.) Assign different unit sizes to each block for even more practice sizing templates.

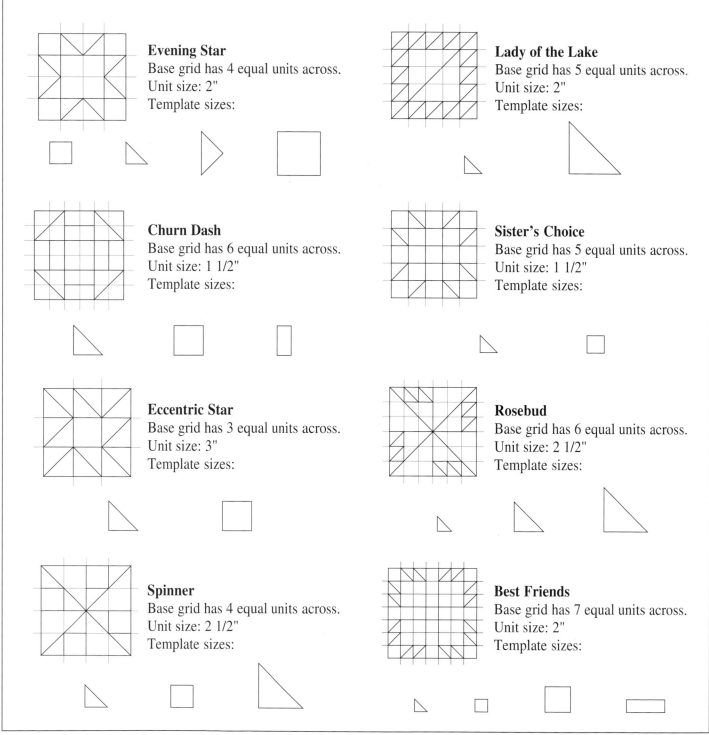

Evening Star
Base grid has 4 equal units across.
Unit size: 2"
Template sizes:

Lady of the Lake
Base grid has 5 equal units across.
Unit size: 2"
Template sizes:

Churn Dash
Base grid has 6 equal units across.
Unit size: 1 1/2"
Template sizes:

Sister's Choice
Base grid has 5 equal units across.
Unit size: 1 1/2"
Template sizes:

Eccentric Star
Base grid has 3 equal units across.
Unit size: 3"
Template sizes:

Rosebud
Base grid has 6 equal units across.
Unit size: 2 1/2"
Template sizes:

Spinner
Base grid has 4 equal units across.
Unit size: 2 1/2"
Template sizes:

Best Friends
Base grid has 7 equal units across.
Unit size: 2"
Template sizes:

Exercise 4

Test Your Drafting Skills

Have fun and test your drafting skills with these blocks. Work with each in a 12" size and follow these steps. 1. Identify the base grid. 2. Determine the unit size for a 12" block. 3. Identify the pattern pieces needed to make the block. 4. Determine the correct size of each piece. (Answers are given on page 60.)

Example

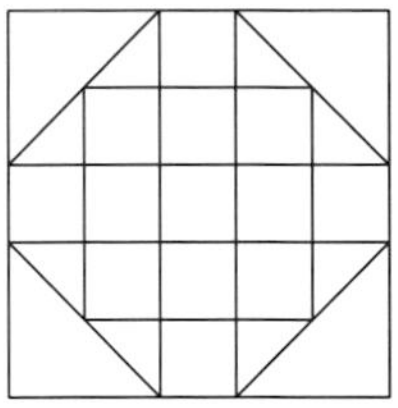

Double Wrench
1. Base grid: _5 equal units across_
2. Unit size: _____2 2/5"_____
3. Pattern pieces needed:

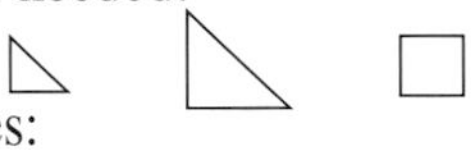

4. Template sizes:

2 2/5"   4 4/5"   2 2/5"

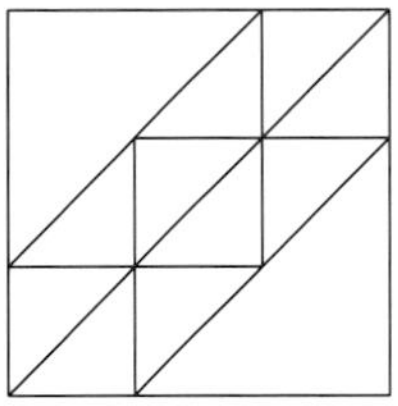

Northwind
1. Base grid: _____
2. Unit size: _____
3. Pattern pieces needed:

4. Template sizes:

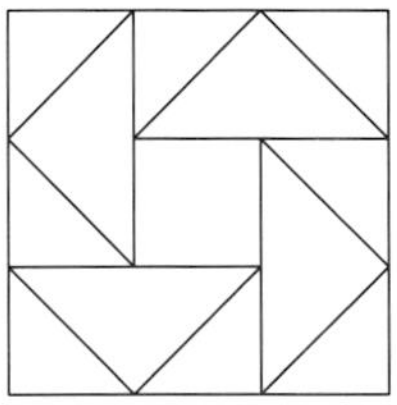

Ribbon
1. Base grid: _____
2. Unit size: _____
3. Pattern pieces needed:

4. Template sizes:

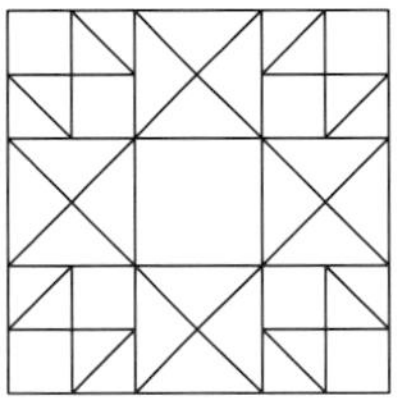

Union Square
1. Base grid: _____
2. Unit size: _____
3. Pattern pieces needed:

4. Template sizes:

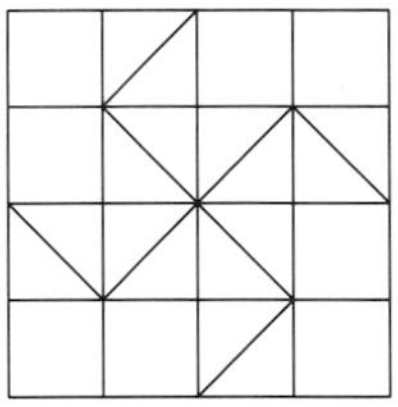

Turnstyle
1. Base grid: _____
2. Unit size: _____
3. Pattern pieces needed:

4. Template sizes:

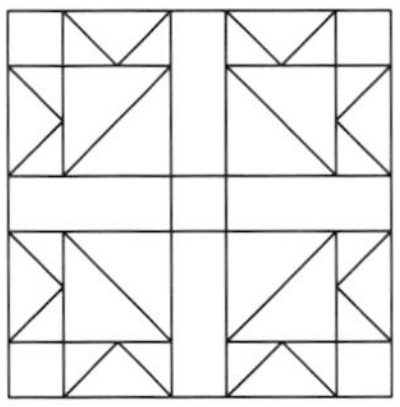

Fourth of July
1. Base grid: _____
2. Unit size: _____
3. Pattern pieces needed:

4. Template sizes:

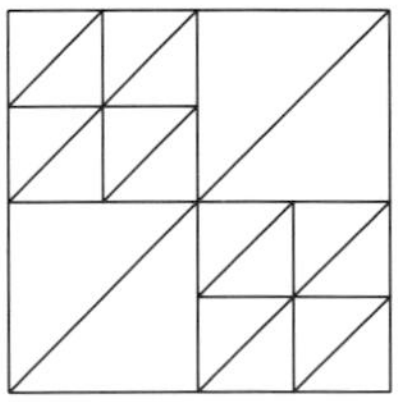

Flock of Geese
1. Base grid: _____
2. Unit size: _____
3. Pattern pieces needed:

4. Template sizes:

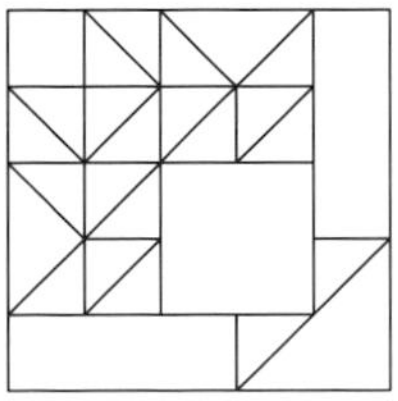

Grape Basket
1. Base grid: _____
2. Unit size: _____
3. Pattern pieces needed:

4. Template sizes:

Exercise 5

Eight-Pointed Stars

Referring to the sample blocks and calculations in Chapter 2, do the calculations for the following blocks to determine the correct sizes for the required templates. Assume that you want a 12" finished block. (Answers are on page 61.)

Flying Bat

Arrowhead Star

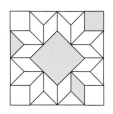

Blazing Star

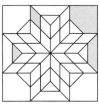

Wood Lily

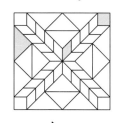

Dutch Rose

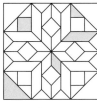

Flying Swallows

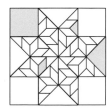

Cutting Aids

Now that you've perfected your drafting skills, you're ready to start working with fabric. In this chapter, we'll examine a number of helpful hints for cutting fabric. First, we will cover cutting fabric with templates using a rotary cutter or scissors. Then, we will look at some of the simpler, more common shapes, and how to cut them without templates. The methods described should help simplify the cutting process and enable you to cut quickly, efficiently and accurately with or without templates.

Cutting Strips

Whether you choose to use templates or not, you will need precut fabric strips to work with. The following guidelines will help you prepare your strips for cutting pieces later on.

First, decide on the grainline orientation for the piece. To determine the width of the strip required for each template, measure your template with the grainline positioned to be in alignment with the grainline of the fabric strip. (Remember, the template includes seam allowances.)

To cut strips fold the fabric in half, selvage to selvage, keeping the fold even and flat. (The raw edges may be somewhat uneven.) Fold the fabric in half once more, making four layers.

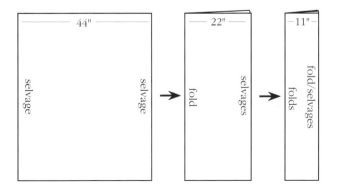

Position the folded fabric on a cutting mat. I prefer mats with grids because the grid lines ensure that my strips will be straight, without "bends" at each fold. Two things cause bends: folding fabric unevenly, and an incorrect angle of the ruler in relationship to the folds of the fabric. The ruler must be absolutely perpendicular to the folds.

Line up the folds with a horizontal line on your cutting mat, approximately 3" up from the bottom edge of the mat. Right-handed people should position the fabric so that it extends to the right. Left-handed people should position the fabric so that it extends to the left.

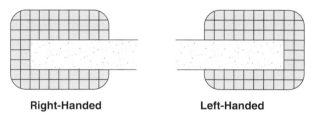

Right-Handed   **Left-Handed**

Align the ruler with a vertical grid line and you will automatically make perpendicular cuts. *NOTE: If your mat does not have grid lines, you can draw two lines on it with a fine-point permanent marker or pen. Make the first line 3" up from the bottom edge of the mat. Make the second line 3" in from the left side of the mat if you are right-handed or 3" in from the right if you are left-handed.*

Begin by eliminating the uneven edges of the fabric, as shown. Place the ruler over the uneven edges, aligning it with a vertical line on the mat. Hold the rotary cutter at a 45° angle to the mat. Make a clean cut through the fabric, beginning in front of the folds and cutting through to the opposite edge with one long, smooth (not short and choppy) stroke. Always cut away from your-self—*never* toward yourself!

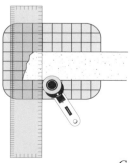

Move the ruler sideways, aligning the edge of the fabric with the proper measurement on the ruler for the strip width desired. The fabric under the ruler will then be the width of the fabric strip you need to cut. Cut the strip as shown.

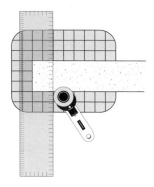

Unfold the fabric strip and check the spots where there were folds. If the fabric was not evenly lined up or the ruler was incorrectly positioned, there will be a bend at each of the folds in the fabric, as shown.

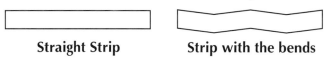

Straight Strip   **Strip with the bends**

Now move the ruler and continue cutting until you have the required number of strips. (To keep the cut edges even, always move the ruler, not the fabric.) When cutting many strips, check after every four or five strips to make sure the strips are straight. Leave the other strips folded in fourths until you are ready to use them.

Cutting With Templates

When you have drafted your block pattern, decided on coloration and made your templates, it is time to cut the pieces. It is difficult and awkward to position a template on a scrap of fabric and then cut around it with the rotary cutter. Positioning the templates on fabric strips of specific widths, as above, will minimize cutting.

Frequently in a given quilt block coloration occurs in fours (four of a given shape for a particular fabric in the block). By folding the fabric into fourths and cutting a strip equal to the width of the template, you will get four pieces from one cut. If you need less than four of any one fabric, just unfold the strip and cut as needed.

Turn the folded strips so that the selvage/fold edge is at the left if you are right-handed and at the right, if left-handed. Cut off the selvage/fold edge with the rotary cutter.

Position the template on the strip so the three straight outside edges of the fabric strip line up with the edges of the template. Use the rotary cutter and cut carefully along the remaining edge(s) of the template.

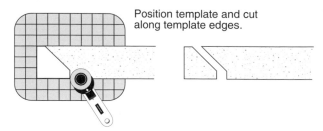

Position template and cut along template edges.

If you are concerned about damaging the edges of your template when cutting, trace the template on the fabric with a fine-tip pen, then lay a ruler along your marked line and cut with the rotary cutter.

If you prefer to cut with scissors, begin by cutting a strip of fabric the desired width. (You may want to use a rotary cutter for this part.) Position the template on the strip, mark around it and cut carefully with scissors. With good, sharp scissors you can cut through multiple layers of fabric. Cut multiple layers on a padded surface. The scissors sink down into the padding and help to keep the four layers even, as opposed to cutting on a hard surface where the layers tend to lift and separate as you cut. (A padded surface can be made from the cardboard center of a bolt of fabric. Wrap a double layer of needlepunch batting around the cardboard. Cover with a layer of cotton fabric and tape it to the back side with packaging tape. This padded surface also makes a wonderful portable ironing board—lightweight and extremely durable.)

Cutting Without Templates

Some shapes can be cut easily and quickly without the use of templates. Such shapes include squares, half-square triangles, quarter-square triangles, rectangles and diamonds. Often, you can combine cutting with and without templates for the same block depending on the shape of the piece you are working with.

Because you must include seam allowance, there is a little bit of math involved in cutting without templates. The following formulas work and provide everything you need to know in order to be able to cut the given shapes without templates.

Squares: Finished size plus 1/2".

Example: For a 2" finished square, cut a fabric strip 2 1/2" wide, turn the ruler and cut a 2 1/2" square.

2 1/2" [rectangle diagram] = 2" finished [square]
2 1/2"

Half-Square Triangles: Finished size of side of triangle plus 7/8".

Example: For a 2" half-square triangle, cut a fabric strip 2 7/8" wide, turn the ruler and cut a 2 7/8" square. Position the ruler along one diagonal and cut the square into two half-square triangles.

2 7/8" [rectangle with diagonal square diagram] = 2" finished [triangle]
2 7/8" 2 7/8"

Quarter-Square Triangles: Finished length of the base of the triangle plus 1 1/4".

Example: For a 2" finished quarter-square triangle, cut a fabric strip 3 1/4" wide, turn the ruler and cut a 3 1/4" square. Cut the square along both diagonals into four quarter-square triangles.

3 1/4" [rectangle with X square diagram] = [triangle] 2" finished
3 1/4" 3 1/4"

Rectangles: Finished size plus 1/2".

Example: For a 2" x 4" rectangle, cut a fabric strip 2 1/2" wide. (Use the smaller measurement for the strip width.) Turn the ruler and cut at 4 1/2" intervals.

2 1/2" [rectangle diagram] = 2" 4" finished
4 1/2" 4 1/2"

Diamonds: Divide the finished size of the side of the diamond by 1.41, then add 1/2" to find the strip width to cut.

Example: For a diamond with 2" sides:
2" ÷ 1.41 = 1.4 + 1/2" = 1.9"

Cut a strip 1.9". Establish a 45° angle. Measure over 1.9" and cut parallel to that 45° angle. *NOTE: I make a 1.9"-wide plastic strip from template plastic, using* *10 squares to the inch graph paper as a measuring guide. Then I can use this plastic strip to measure and cut my 1.9"-wide strips.*

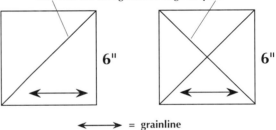

1.9" [strip diagram with 1.9" and 45° lines] = 2" finished [diamond]

Setting Triangles

I find it extremely helpful to cut without templates when cutting side and corner triangles for quilts with blocks set on point. The logical assumption is to cut squares, the same size as your blocks, diagonally in half to make the right size triangles. For example, a quilt made of 6" finished blocks set on point would need 6" half-square triangles for the sides and 6" quarter-square triangles would work for the corners. However, if you use the preceding guidelines, you will cut triangles with bias edges along the entire outside edge of the quilt.

Bias will run along outside edge of quilt.

[two 6" square diagrams with diagonals and grainline arrows]
6"   6"

⟷ = grainline

In order to get the straight grain along the outside edge of the quilt, you need to convert the side triangle to a quarter-square triangle, and the corner triangle to a half-square triangle. Let's look at a quilt with 6" blocks set on point.

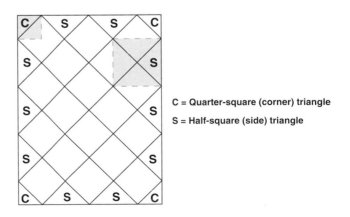

C = Quarter-square (corner) triangle

S = Half-square (side) triangle

By using the "1.41" number and converting each triangle, you will have straight grain all along the outside edge:

A 6" half-square triangle converts to a quarter-square triangle by multiplying by 1.41:

$$6" \times 1.41 = 8.46"$$

8.46" = the base measurement of the quarter-square triangle you will need. Adust the decimal to a more workable fraction—8 1/2", and add 1 1/4" (9 3/4") according to the formula for quarter-square triangles. Cut a 9 3/4" square and cut diagonally from corner to corner in both directions for four quarter-square triangles. These triangles will fit along the sides of the quilt and have straight grain where needed.

Therefore, the rule for cutting quarter-square triangles (with the grainline running along the long side of the triangle) is: *find the finished measurement needed for the long side of the triangle and add 1 1/4" (for seam allowances).*

A 6" quarter-square triangle converts to a half-square triangle by dividing by 1.41:

$$6" \div 1.41 = 4.25"$$

4.25" = the side measurement of the half-square triangle you will need. To 4 1/4" add 7/8" (5 1/8") according to the formula for half-square triangles. Cut a 5 1/8" square and cut diagonally in half from corner to corner for two half-square triangles with straight grain where needed.

Therefore, the rule for cutting half-square triangles (with the grainline running along the short side of the triangle) is: *find the finished measurement needed for the short side of the triangle and add 7/8".*

Keep the following chart handy for cutting side and corner setting triangles without templates.

Original Triangle Measurement	Square for new Side Setting Triangle	Square for new Corner Setting Triangle
6" △ or △	9 3/4" ⊠	5 1/8" ◹
7" △ or △	11 1/8" ⊠	6 1/8" ◹
8" △ or △	12 1/2" ⊠	6 1/2" ◹
9" △ or △	14" ⊠	7 1/4" ◹
10" △ or △	15 1/4" ⊠	7 7/8" ◹
11" △ or △	16 3/4" ⊠	8 2/3" ◹
12" △ or △	18 1/8" ⊠	9 3/8" ◹

Quick and Easy Yardage Calculations

If you cut your pieces from templates, as described earlier in this chapter, the following hints will

help in determining yardage requirements. Calculations are based on the assumption that strips are cut selvage to selvage and left folded in fourths before cutting the pattern pieces. All cutting is done through four layers at a time. To simplify the math, calculations will be based on how many pieces can be cut from a 10" strip. Multiply that number by four (the number of fabric layers) to determine the exact yield per 40"-42" strip.

First, decide on the grainline orientation for the piece. Then, with the grainline running along the edge of the ruler, measure the height of the pattern pieces, including seam allowances.

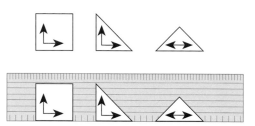

This measurement determines how wide to make the strips from which you will cut the particular pieces. Remember, the fabric is folded in fourths, so each cut will yield four pieces. For the calculations, plan on 10" of usable fabric (a 40"-42" strip folded in fourths). If your fabrics are wider or narrower than 42", you will need to adjust accordingly.

Now determine how many pieces will fit across the 10" strip. Some shapes, like squares and rectangles, are easy to work with. You can do the calculations using the finished length of the piece plus 1/2" (seam allowance). For example, do the following calculations to figure yardage for a finished 2" square.

A 10" strip will yield:
$$10" \div 2\ 1/2" = 4 \text{ squares}$$

And 4 x 4 (layers of fabric) = 16, 2" finished squares per 40-42" strip.

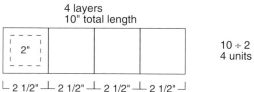

4 layers
10" total length

10 ÷ 2 1/2 = 4 cut units
4 units x 4 layers = 16 total

2 1/2" 2 1/2" 2 1/2" 2 1/2"

Triangles are a bit more complicated. Probably the easiest way to find out how many triangles fit across the 10" strip is to trace the template on a piece of graph paper 10" long to determine the actual yield.

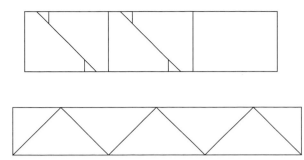

Yardage for half-square triangles can be figured by allowing the finished length of the triangle plus 1 1/4". Two, 2" finished half-square triangles will fit in a 3 1/4" length, as shown.

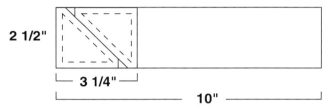

Thus, a 10" strip will yield:

10" ÷ 3 1/4" = 3 x 2 triangles = 6 cut triangles

And 6 x 4 (the strip is folded in fourths) = 24 triangles per 40–42" strip.

Figuring yardage for quarter-square triangles can be a bit confusing. It is helpful to know that the maximum finished-size quarter-square triangle that will fit three across the 10" strip, as illustrated, is a 4" finished triangle.

When you have quarter-square triangles larger than 4" finished, you may find it more fabric-efficient to unfold the strip once so you are cutting across a 20" length. If you wish, you may position two strips together so you are still cutting through four layers.

4 Layers

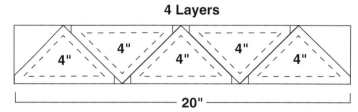

Again, the simplest way to figure yardage for many shapes is simply to draw around that shape on graph paper and count. That removes both the doubt and the math!

Once you know how many pieces a 10" strip will yield, and you know the total number of pieces you need for your quilt, then you can figure the total number of strips needed.

Multiply the number of strips needed by the height of the strip for the total yardage needed in inches. Pad this number by 1/8 to 1/4 yard to allow for loss in folding. It is better to have too much fabric than too little. ◢

TLC for Rotary Cutters

CHAPTER V

The Rotary Cutter Revolution

It was early in the 1980s when rotary cutters were introduced to the quilt world, revolutionizing the way quilters cut their fabric. My first experiences with rotary cutters were not always positive. To save money, I bought the small cutter instead of the large cutter. Later, someone persuaded me to invest in a large wheel, a definite improvement. Still there were problems. No one ever showed me the correct way to use a cutter. I would get crooked strips. I would find I hadn't cut through the fold edges at the start of cutting. The ruler would move as I pushed against it while cutting across the fabric. I didn't know at what angle to hold the cutter or which direction the cutter should face. These things can make a big difference, and if you aren't comfortable and successful, then you won't want to use a rotary cutter. I also thought that using a rotary cutter was only for cutting your pieces without a template. Not so!

In teaching I have found that if I take time at the beginning of a workshop to instruct people in some TLC techniques for their rotary cutters, my life as a teacher is easier because I don't have to do a lot of mini-demos later on. Also, people who would be shy about asking for help truly appreciate it. No matter how experienced people are with rotary cutters, they usually learn at least one new thing.

Rotary Cutter Maintenance

For example, do you know that you should *clean and oil* your cutter periodically? When you first purchased your cutter there was a tiny bit of oil that helped to lubricate the cutting wheel, enabling it to turn smoothly and easily. As you cut your fabric, lint collects between the blade and the black plastic piece it rolls against (Figure 1). That lint dries out the oil and impedes the wheel's ability to turn easily. As a result, you must push harder with each cut. Have you ever thought that the cutter used to feel easier to use than it does today? Maybe you just thought the blade was getting a bit dull so you replaced it. At $6.00 a blade, that can get expensive.

Sometimes cleaning and oiling are all the cutter needs to begin acting like a brand new cutter. Chang-

ing a blade and not oiling it makes it "feel" dull. If you have a nick in your blade (you dropped the cutter, you accidentally cut the ruler, etc.), then you will need to replace the blade. (Unfortunately, sometimes you get defective blades right from the package. Don't try to use bad blades. The frustration and the problems you'll incur are not worth it.)

When you buy a new blade for your cutter it frequently has a bit of oil on it. I've lost count of the number of quilters who told me that they wiped the oil off before putting the blade on! Please don't do that. In fact, promise yourself that every time you use your cutter a lot (once a day, once a week, or once a month) you will take the time to take it apart to clean out all that lint and add a fresh drop of oil.

Getting to Know Your Rotary Cutter

Don't stop reading now for fear that once you take that cutter apart you might never get it together again. Keep reading! I used to share your fear: would I ever remember how all those pieces fit together if I took it apart? Actually, the first time I took my cutter apart, I *couldn't* get it back together. I went out and bought a whole new cutter just to figure the system out. I will give you some pointers about rotary assem-

Figure 1. Yuck! If your rotary cutter has never been cleaned and you use it often, it probably looks like this.

Figure 2. Some rotary cutters have small, cupped washers, others have large, flat ones.

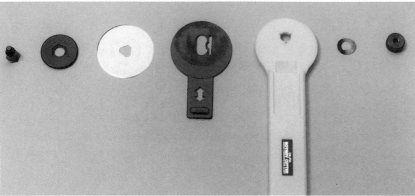

Figure 3. One of the oldest Olfa rotary cutters.

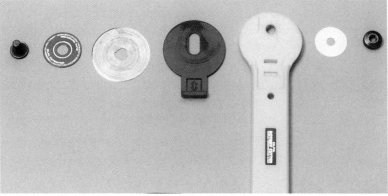

Figure 4. Another one of the older Olfa rotary cutters.

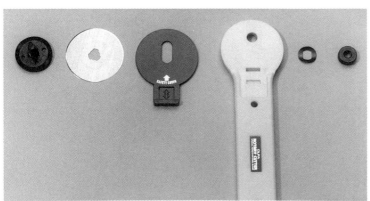

Figure 5. One of the newer Olfa rotary cutters.

bly that should allay your fears and perhaps save you the expense of buying a new cutter.

There are several brands of cutters on the market. The most common brand I see is Olfa, then Kai or Dritz. Quilter's Rule also has their own brand of rotary cutter. One of the newer cutters is made by Fiskars. I'm sure there are others as well. Each cutter is just a little bit different, each with pros and cons. Over the years there have been changes made to the cutters' parts, presumably to make them better, more efficient and easier to put together. The absence of assembly directions on the replacement blade packaging was very frustrating to me until I realized how many different cutter configurations there actually are.

All cutters have the same basic parts: **handle** (yellow for Olfa, gray for Kai, brown for Dritz—unless you have one of the novelty colored ones, turquoise or fuchsia, that were made for a while—and blue for Quilter's Rule). The **blade** you know. Most cutters have some sort of **washer** (Figure 2); it may be large and flat or small and cupped. (It's supposed to be that way; don't try to flatten it!) Kai/Dritz has no washer. There will be a **screw**, a **nut** and maybe, depending on the cutter, a **disk** to get the tension right. The two older Olfa cutters, Quilter's Rule and Fiskars also have tension disks, flat metal pieces with words or a black plastic disk (orange, for Fiskars); neither the Kai/Dritz nor the newest Olfa cutters have these tension disks. The disk lies on top of the blade; the screw goes through the disk hole. The tension factor has been built into the screw so people won't have to worry about that part. Each cutter also has a black plastic **shield**, which goes between the blade and the handle.

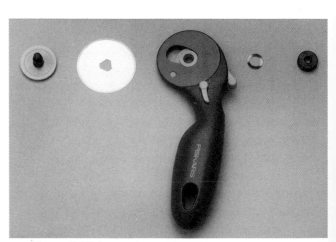

Figure 6. Fiskars rotary cutter.

I've disassembled all the rotary cutters mentioned above and photographed them for your reference (Figures 3-8). It's easier to keep track of all the various parts by laying them out in the order in which they go together. Find the picture of your rotary cutter, and carefully take yours apart, referring to the photograph as needed. Watch out for the little cupped washers (if your rotary cutter has one). They can go flying off without warning, never to be found! Use a tissue to wipe everything off. If you have any rust spots on your blade, which happens in damp climates, I recommend changing the blade. Oiling it frequently will reduce rusting. Be sure to remove any spots where lint has dried and hardened onto the blade or the black plastic shield. Those spots definitely affect the cutter's ability to work properly. Once you have cleaned everything you are ready to reassemble the cutter.

Start with the handle right side up—the side the blade goes on. (The Quilter's Rule cutter can be assembled for right-handed or left-handed use, so be sure to position it as you need it. For right-handed assembly of the Quilter's Rule the handle will be angled like a backwards C when the blade is at the top.) Next, place the black plastic shield on top of the handle, positioning the bottom of the oval opening even with the round opening in the handle (Olfa and Quilter's Rule); Kai/Dritz has a round opening on both pieces. Put one **drop** of sewing machine oil on the black plastic guide below the opening (Figure 9). For the Kai/Dritz you may want to work 2–3 drops of oil around with a cotton swab (Figure 10). The black plastic guide for this cutter has a large donut-shaped end that needs more attention in order for the oil to spread thoroughly. For the other cutters, the one drop will be dispersed evenly once cutting begins.

Figure 9. To oil your Olfa, Quilter's Rule or Fiskars rotary cutter, place one drop of sewing machine oil on the black plastic guide below the opening.

Figure 10. To oil your Kai/Dritz rotary cutter, work 2-3 drops of oil around the black plastic guide with a cotton swab.

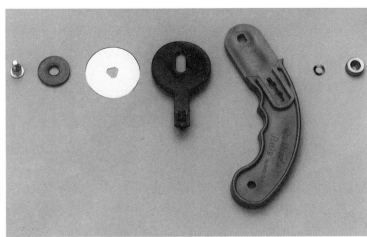

Figure 7. Quilter's Rule rotary cutter.

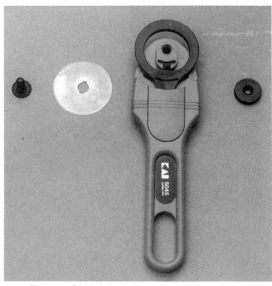

Figure 8. Kai/Dritz rotary cutter.

Next replace the blade, being sure to center it on the black guide (the protected state). Please be careful not to cut yourself! Now comes the fun part, where the cutters are all different. For those with a tension disk, the disk has a groove in which to seat the screw. Old Olfas have a hexagon-shaped groove which fits the hexagon-shaped screw.* Quilter's Rule and Fiskars have a round space for round screws. Be sure to seat everything securely or you will have a wobbly cutter. *NOTE: *The opening on the black plastic shield of the old Olfa cutter with the hexagon-shaped screw has more than a plain oval; it has a thin plastic guide which sometimes breaks after usage. It is common to find that even with one end broken the cutter still works. Eventually both ends break loose. When this happens, the action becomes quite sloppy and you will probably need to replace the cutter. This is why Olfa no longer makes this kind of opening.*

Once the screw and tension disk (if your cutter has one) are in position through the blade, black plastic guide and handle, turn the cutter over and put the washer on. If your washer is cupped, position the washer so that it now cups **up** (with your rotary cutter blade down). The washer hole probably will have at least one flat edge, sometimes two, that will match the shape of the screw. If your washer is flat, it makes no difference which side is up. Everything must fit for your cutter to operate smoothly. Remember, the Kai/Dritz has no washer.

Finally, replace the nut. If your washer is flat, the nut will have one flat side and one curved side. Be sure to position the curved side against the washer. If your washer is cupped, the nut will have one flat side and one side that looks hollowed out. Put the nut on flat side up. Don't over-tighten the nut. If it is too tight it will affect the cutting action. The blade should turn smoothly and easily without being *pushed*. The action of cutting should be more a feeling that you are *guiding* rather than pushing the cutter. The harder you have to work, the more likely you are to have some of those problems I referred to earlier (i.e. rulers that slip).

◢ In a Nutshell

Clean and oil your cutters frequently. When reassembling your cutter, put the blade on top of the black plastic shield. If your washer is cupped put it on "cup up;" if your washer is flat place the round edge of the nut against the washer. Don't tighten the nut too much. *And, ALWAYS remember to lock the blade cover in place whenever you set down your rotary cutter, even if it's just for a moment.* Note that the blade cover on the Dritz cutter does not lock in place. With even the slightest amount of pressure, the blade can be exposed to unknowing fingers!

When I include TLC for rotary cutters in my workshops, people tell me that the information has paid for the workshop, saving them blades and frustration. I do hope you find the information useful. Remember to take care of your tools. If you do, you'll find that they will work with you, not against you! ◢

Conclusion

By now, I hope you're feeling very satisfied with yourself. I'll bet you're surprised at how simple the whole drafting process is! Once you stop saying "I can't" and just do it, anything is possible.

I also hope you have taken the time to practice cutting with templates, as outlined in Chapter 4. I have found that as people actually try the technique, they are amazed at how easy and accurate it is—not to mention faster. When you don't have to worry about looking for numbers and angles on your rotary ruler; you can whiz through the cutting phase. And, the more you practice, the simpler the process will become.

In closing, I would like to share a favorite quote. It was given to me by one of my adult education students a number of years ago. We don't know who the author is, but I think it sums up this whole process.

> "Accomplishment does not reside in repeating the past newly, just as painting by numbers doesn't produce art. Accomplishment is born of risk—of the courage to step beyond what's comfortable, predictable or known."

Remember, "knowledge is freedom." To obtain knowledge one must venture out of the safe, comfortable and familiar. Gaining knowledge may also hurt, but the results are worth it. Your personal satisfaction with the quilts you will produce will make it all worthwhile.

Sample Blocks

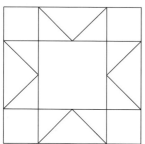

Variable Star

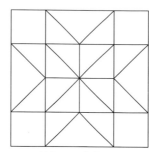

Pieced Star

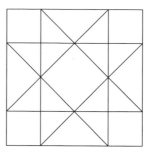

Evening Star

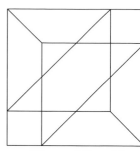

Star of David

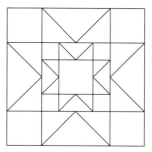

Star within a Star

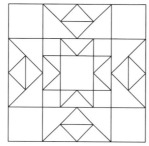

Star in the Middle

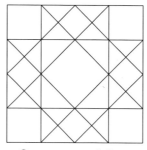

Square and Star

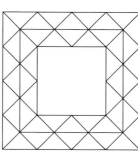

Ocean Waves

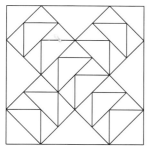

Railroad Crossing

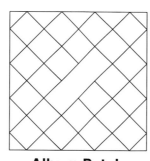

Album Patch

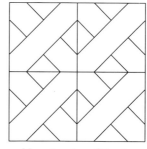

Kentucky Chain

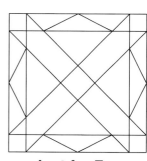

Just for Fun

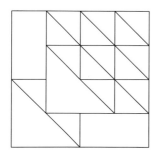

Basket

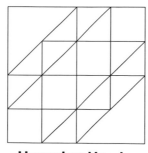

Hovering Hawks

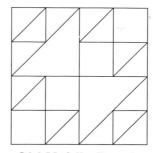

Old Maid's Puzzle

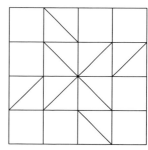

Clay's Choice

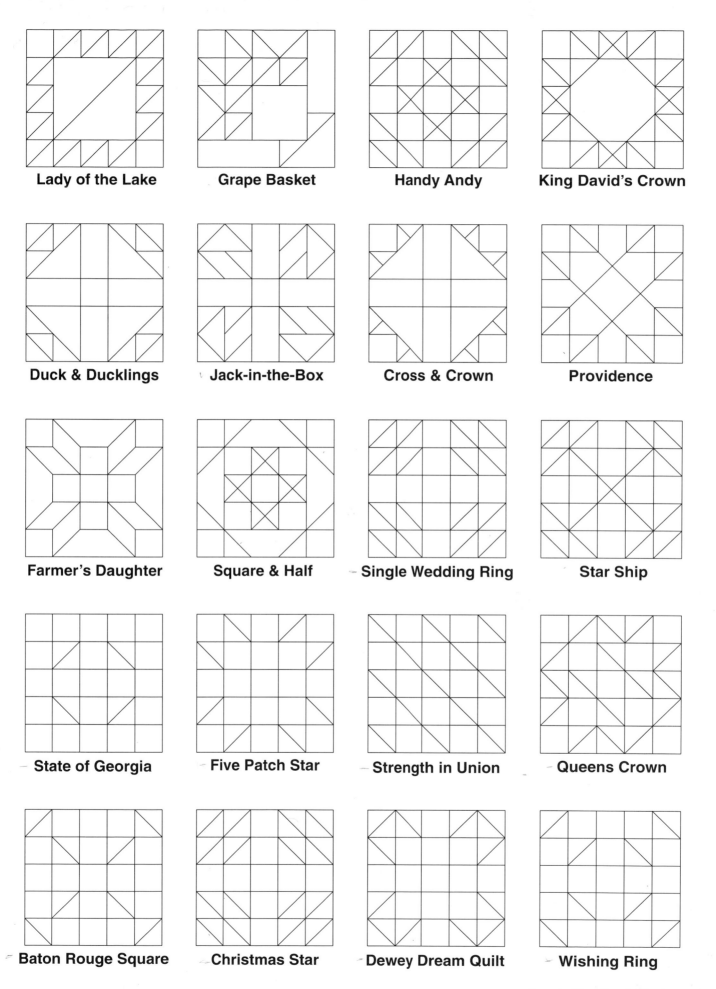

Lady of the Lake   **Grape Basket**   **Handy Andy**   **King David's Crown**

Duck & Ducklings   **Jack-in-the-Box**   **Cross & Crown**   **Providence**

Farmer's Daughter   **Square & Half**   **Single Wedding Ring**   **Star Ship**

State of Georgia   **Five Patch Star**   **Strength in Union**   **Queens Crown**

Baton Rouge Square   **Christmas Star**   **Dewey Dream Quilt**   **Wishing Ring**

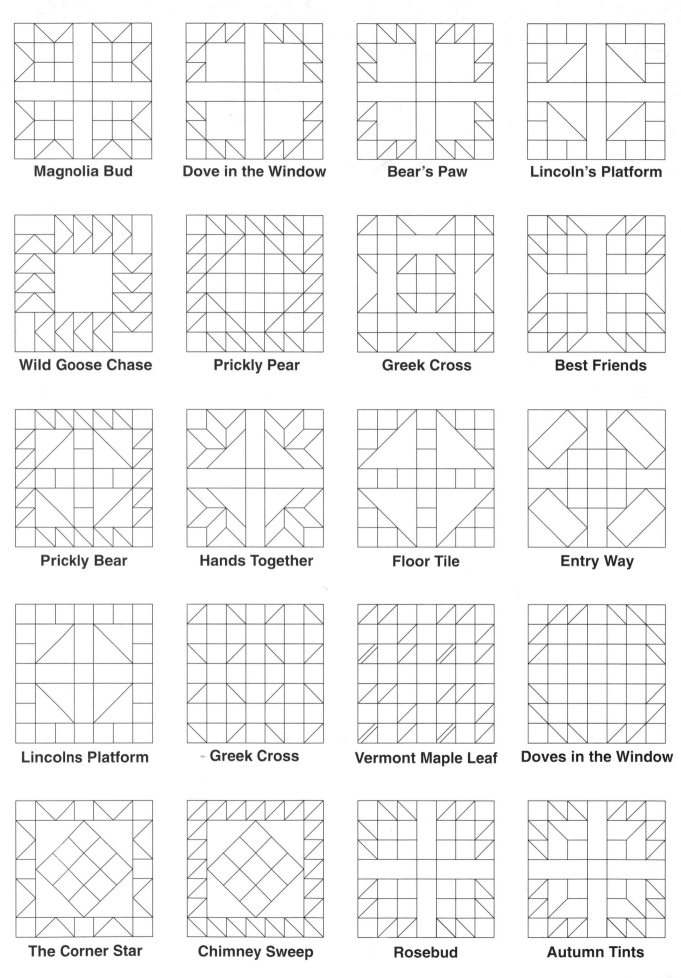

Magnolia Bud **Dove in the Window** **Bear's Paw** **Lincoln's Platform**

Wild Goose Chase **Prickly Pear** **Greek Cross** **Best Friends**

Prickly Bear **Hands Together** **Floor Tile** **Entry Way**

Lincolns Platform **- Greek Cross** **Vermont Maple Leaf** **Doves in the Window**

The Corner Star **Chimney Sweep** **Rosebud** **Autumn Tints**

56   *Sample Seven-Patch Blocks*

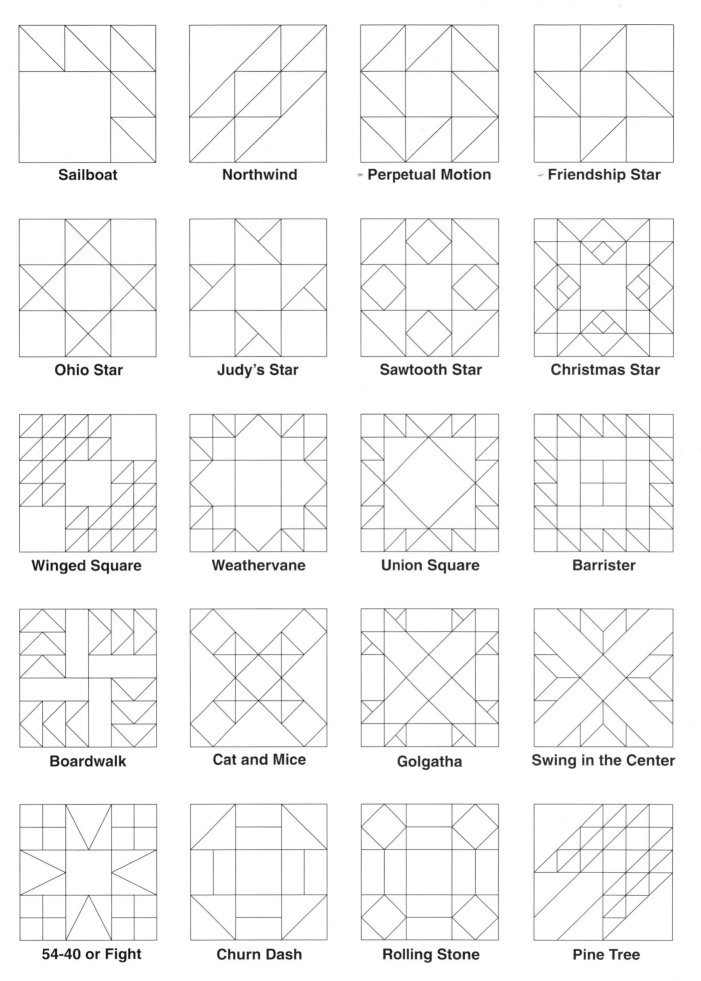

Sailboat **Northwind** ▸ **Perpetual Motion** ▸ **Friendship Star**

Ohio Star **Judy's Star** **Sawtooth Star** **Christmas Star**

Winged Square **Weathervane** **Union Square** **Barrister**

Boardwalk **Cat and Mice** **Golgatha** **Swing in the Center**

54-40 or Fight **Churn Dash** **Rolling Stone** **Pine Tree**

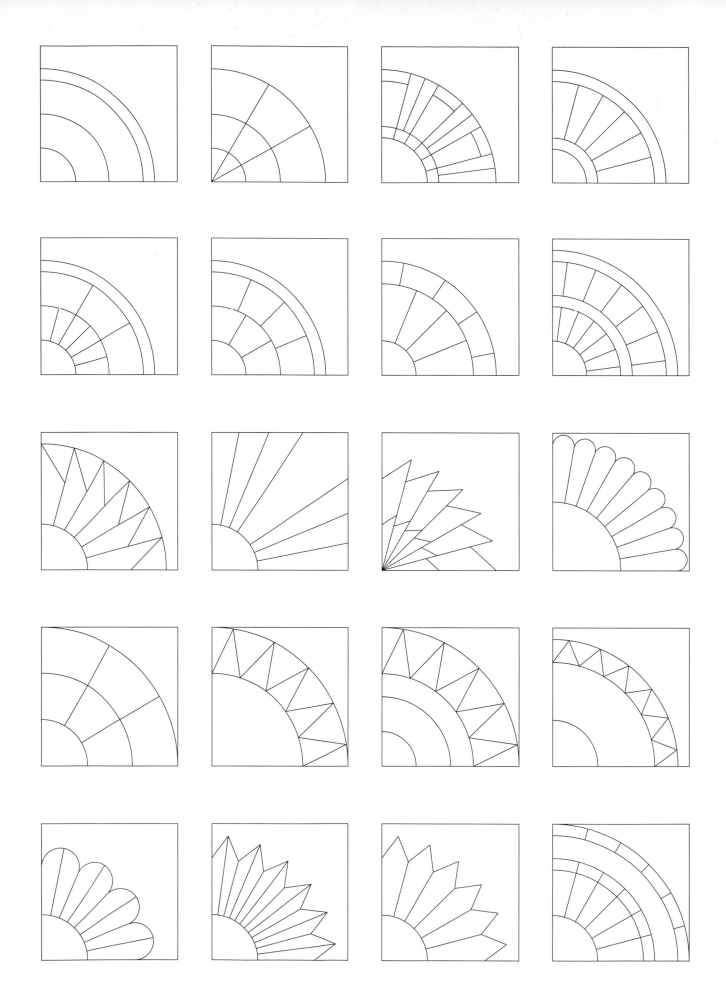

Appendix B

Exercise Answers

Exercise 1
Identifying Base Grids

Evening Star
4 equal units across
4–patch

Eccentric Star
3 equal units across
9–patch

Lady of the Lake
5 equal units across
5–patch

Rosebud
6 equal units across
9–patch

Churn Dash
3 equal units across
9–patch

Spinner
4 equal units across
4–patch

Sister's Choice
5 equal units across
5–patch

Best Friends
7 equal units across
7–patch

Exercise 2
Drafting Blocks in Different Sizes

Evening Star
Base grid has **4** equal units across.
Unit size for a 12" block: **3"**
1 1/2" units = **6"** block
2" units = **8"** block
2 1/2" units = **10"** block

Star Within a Star
Base grid has **8** equal units across.
Unit size for a 12" block: **1 1/2"**
1" units = **8"** block
2" units = **16"** block
2 1/2" units = **20"** block

Churn Dash
Base grid has **3** equal units across.
Unit size for a 12" block: **4"**
1 1/2" units = **4 1/2"** block
2" units = **6"** block
2 1/2" units = **7 1/2"** block

Swing in the Center
Base grid has **6** equal units across.
Unit size for a 12" block: **2"**
1" units = **6"** block
1 1/2" units = **9"** block
3 1/2" units = **21"** block

Wheels
Base grid has **4** equal units across.
Unit size for a 12" block: **3"**
1" units = **4"** block
2" units = **8"** block
3 1/2" units = **14"** block

Jack-in-the-Box
Base grid has **5** equal units across.
Unit size for a 12" block: **2.4"**
1 1/2" units = **7 1/2"** block
2" units = **10"** block
3" units = **15"** block

Boardwalk
Base grid has **6** equal units across.
Unit size for a 12" block: **2"**
1 1/2" units = **9"** block
2 1/2" units = **15"** block
3" units = **18"** block

Hands Together
Base grid has **7** equal units across.
Unit size for a 12" block: **1.71"**
1 1/2" units = **10 1/2"** block
2" units = **14"** block
2 1/2" units = **17 1/2"** block

Exercise 3
Template Sizing

Evening Star
Base grid has 4 equal units across.
Unit size: 2"
Template sizes:

2" ▢   4" ▢   ◮ 4"   2" ◺

Churn Dash
Base grid has 6 equal units across.
Unit size: 1 1/2"
Template sizes:

3" ◺   3" ▢   1 1/2" ▭ 3"

Eccentric Star
Base grid has 3 equal units across.
Unit size: 3"
Template sizes:

3" ◺   3" ▢

Spinner
Base grid has 4 equal units across.
Unit size: 2 1/2"
Template sizes:

2 1/2" ◺   5" ◺   2 1/2" ▢

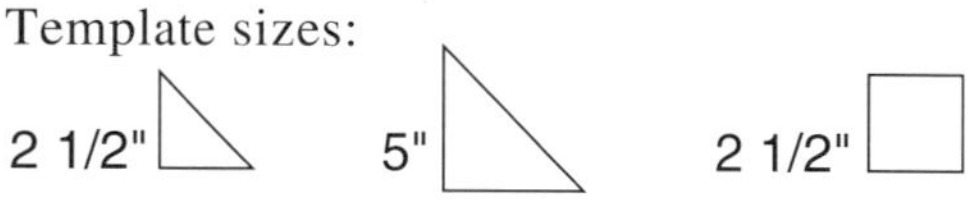

Lady of the Lake
Base grid has 5 equal units across.
Unit size: 2"
Template sizes:

2" ◺   6" ◺

Sister's Choice
Base grid has 5 equal units across.
Unit size: 1 1/2"
Template sizes:

1 1/2" ◺   1 1/2" ▢

Rosebud
Base grid has 6 equal units across.
Unit size: 2 1/2"
Template sizes:

2 1/2" ◺   5" ◺   7 1/2" ◺

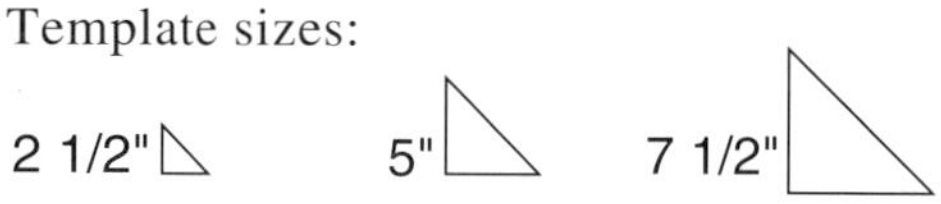

Best Friends
Base grid has 7 equal units across.
Unit size: 2"
Template sizes:

2" ◺   2" ▢   4" ▢   2" ▭ 4"

Exercise 4
Test Your Drafting Skills

Double Wrench
1. Base grid: 5 equal units across
2. Unit size: 2 2/5"
3. Pattern pieces needed:

◺   ◺   ▢

4. Template sizes:

2 2/5" ◺   4 4/5" ◺   2 2/5" ▢

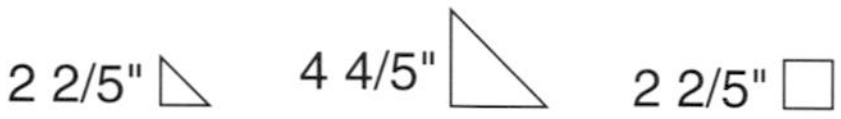

Ribbon
1. Base grid: 3 equal units across
2. Unit size: 4"
3. Pattern pieces needed:

◺   △   ▢

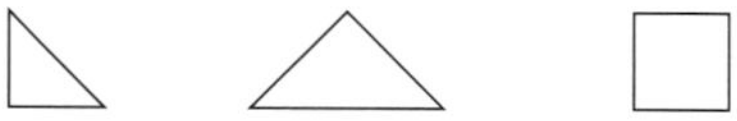

4. Template sizes:

4" ◺   △ 8"   4" ▢

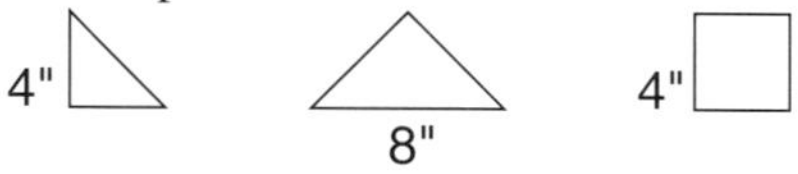

Turnstyle
1. Base grid: 4 equal units across
2. Unit size: 3"
3. Pattern pieces needed:

◺   ▢

4. Template sizes:

3" ◺   3" ▢

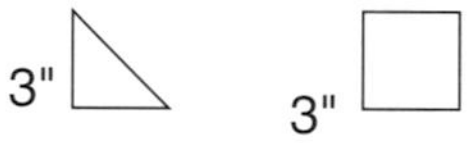

Flock of Geese
1. Base grid: 4 equal units across
2. Unit size: 3"
3. Pattern pieces needed:

◺   ◺

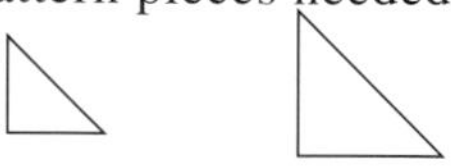

4. Template sizes:

3" ◺   6" ◺

Exercise 4
Test Your Drafting Skills

Northwind
1. Base grid: 3 equal units across
2. Unit size: 4"
3. Pattern pieces needed:

4. Template sizes:

4"　　　8"

Union Square
1. Base grid: 6 equal units across
2. Unit size: 2"
3. Pattern pieces needed:

4. Template sizes:

2" 　　2" 　4"
2" □ 　 △4"　 2"□ 　 4"□

Fourth of July
1. Base grid: 7 equal units across
2. Unit size: 1 5/7"
3. Pattern pieces needed:

4. Template sizes:

1 5/7"　3 3/7"　△3 3/7"　1 5/7"　5 1/7"　1 5/7"

Grape Basket
1. Base grid: 5 equal units across
2. Unit size: 2 2/5"

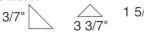

4. Template sizes:

2 2/5" □　2 2/5"　△4 4/5"　2 2/5"　7 1/5"　4 4/5"

Exercise 5
Eight-Pointed Stars

Flying Bat
12" ÷ 3.41= 3.5 = 3 1/2" □
3 1/2"
3 1/2" ÷ 3 = 1.167 = 1 1/6"◇
1 1/6" x 2 = 2 1/3"◇

Blazing Star
12" ÷ 3.41= 3.52 = 3 1/2"
3.5" ÷ 2 = 1.75 = 1 3/4"◇
1 3/4"

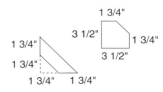

Dutch Rose
12" ÷ 3.41= 3.52 = 3 1/2"
3.5" ÷ 2= 1.75 = 1 3/4"
1 3/4" □
1 3/4" ◇

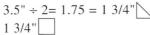

Arrowhead Star
12" ÷ 4.82= 2.49 = 2 1/2" □
2 1/2"◇
2 1/2"
5" □

Flying Swallows
12" ÷ 3.41 = 3.52 = 3 1/2" □
3 1/2"
3.5" ÷ 2.41 = 1.45 = 1 1/2"
1 1/2"◇

Wood Lily
6" x 1.41 = 8.46 ÷ 5.41 = 1.56"
If you adjust the 1.56 down to 1 1/2", you will have
the following templates:
1 1/2"◇
1 1/2" □
3"
11 1/2" block

If you adjust the 1.56 up to 1.6, you will have the
following templates:
1 6/10"◇
1 6/10" □
3 1/5"
12 1/4" block

Master Templates

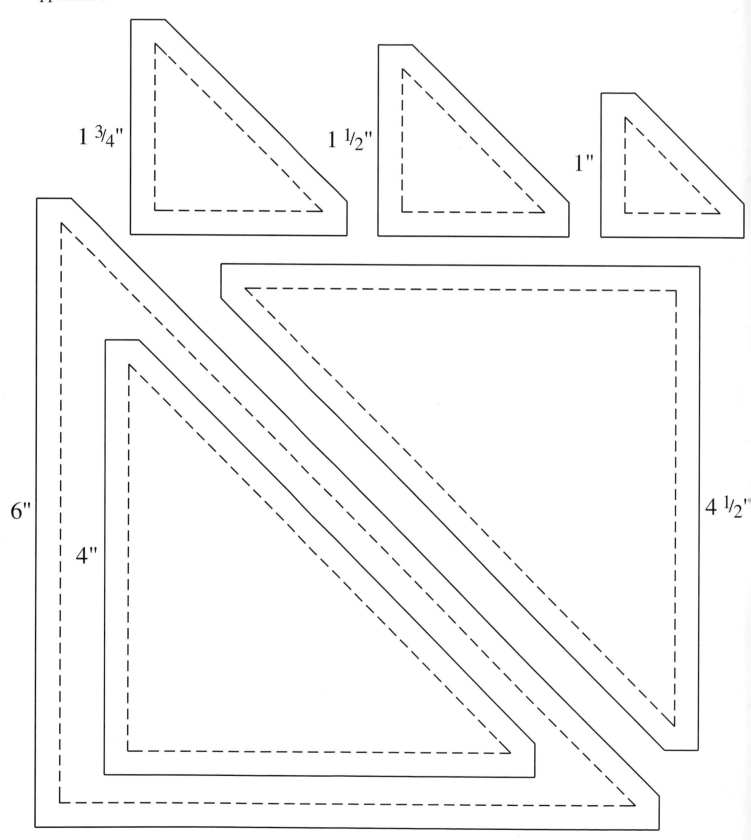

1 ³/₄"

1 ¹/₂"

1"

6"

4"

4 ¹/₂"

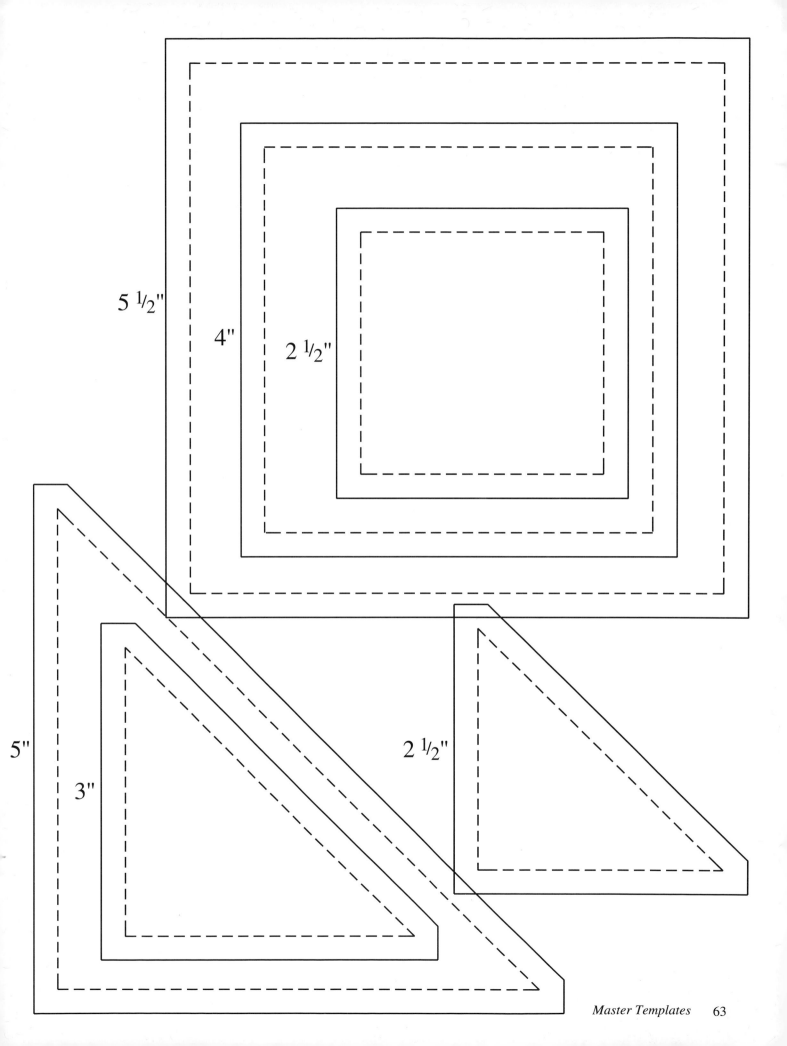

5 ¹/₂"

4"

2 ¹/₂"

5"

3"

2 ¹/₂"

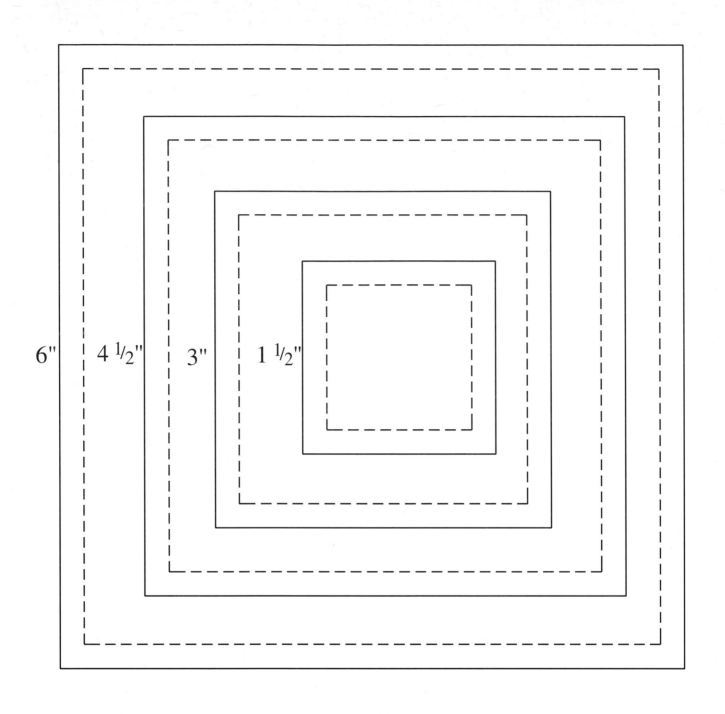

6" 4 ½" 3" 1 ½"

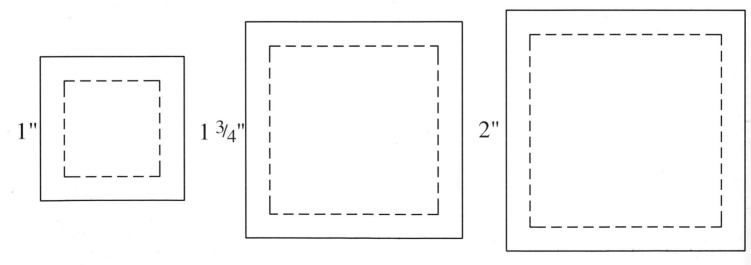

1" 1 ¾" 2"

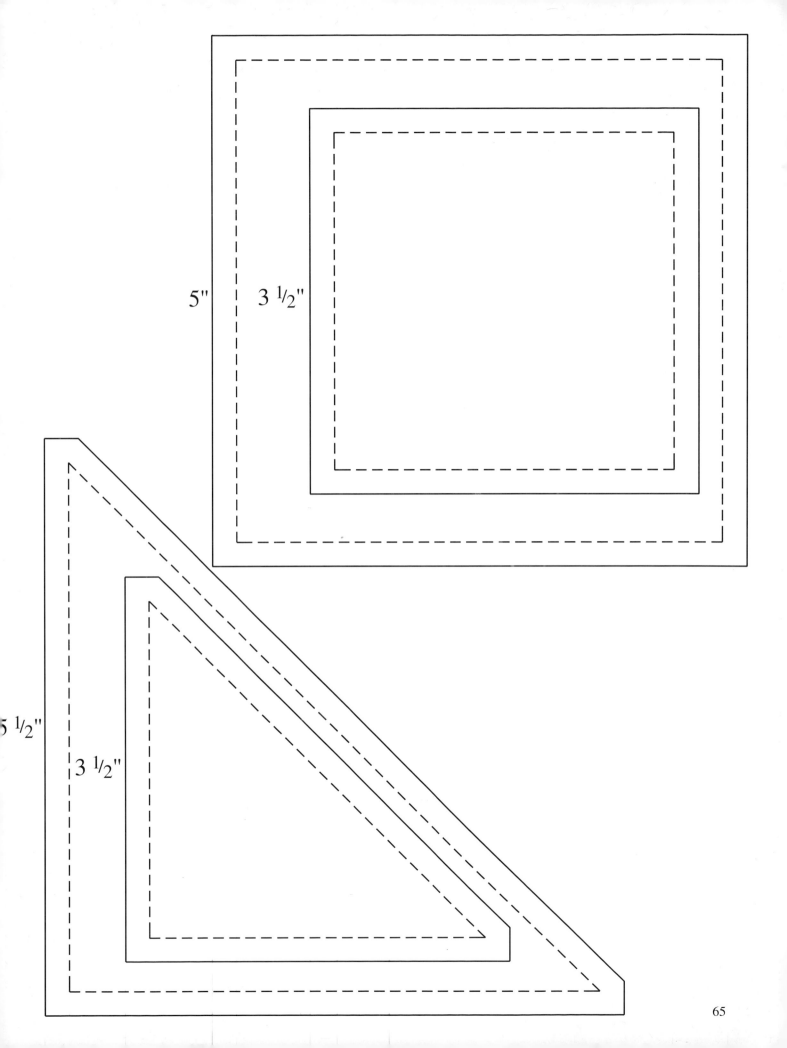

5"

3 ¹/₂"

5 ¹/₂"

3 ¹/₂"

65

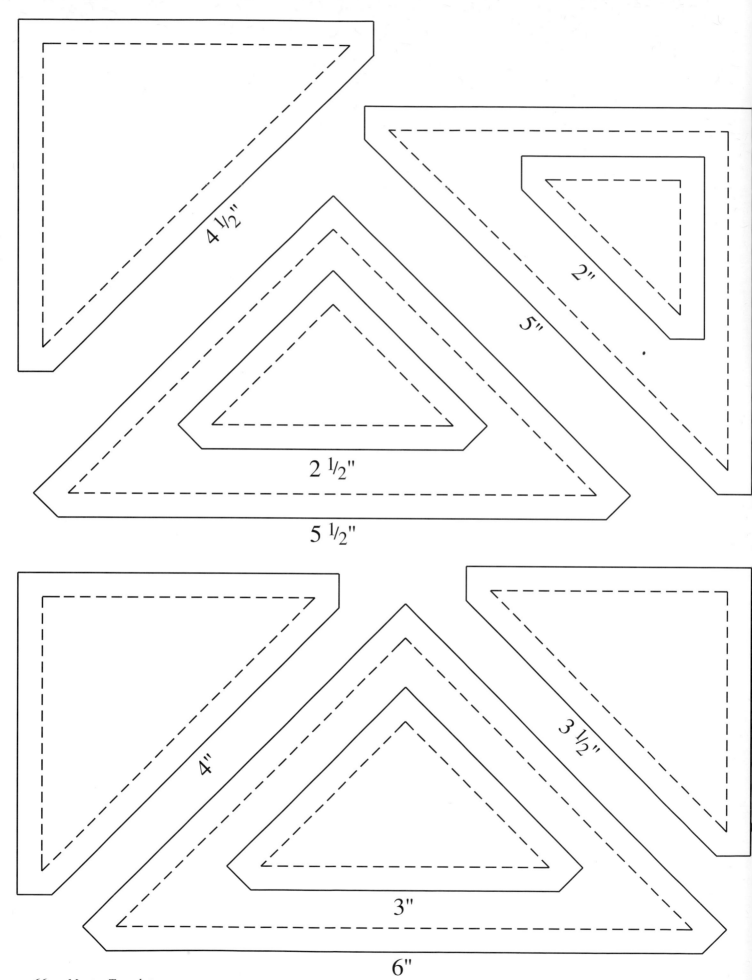

4 ½"

2"

5"

2 ½"

5 ½"

4"

3 ½"

3"

6"

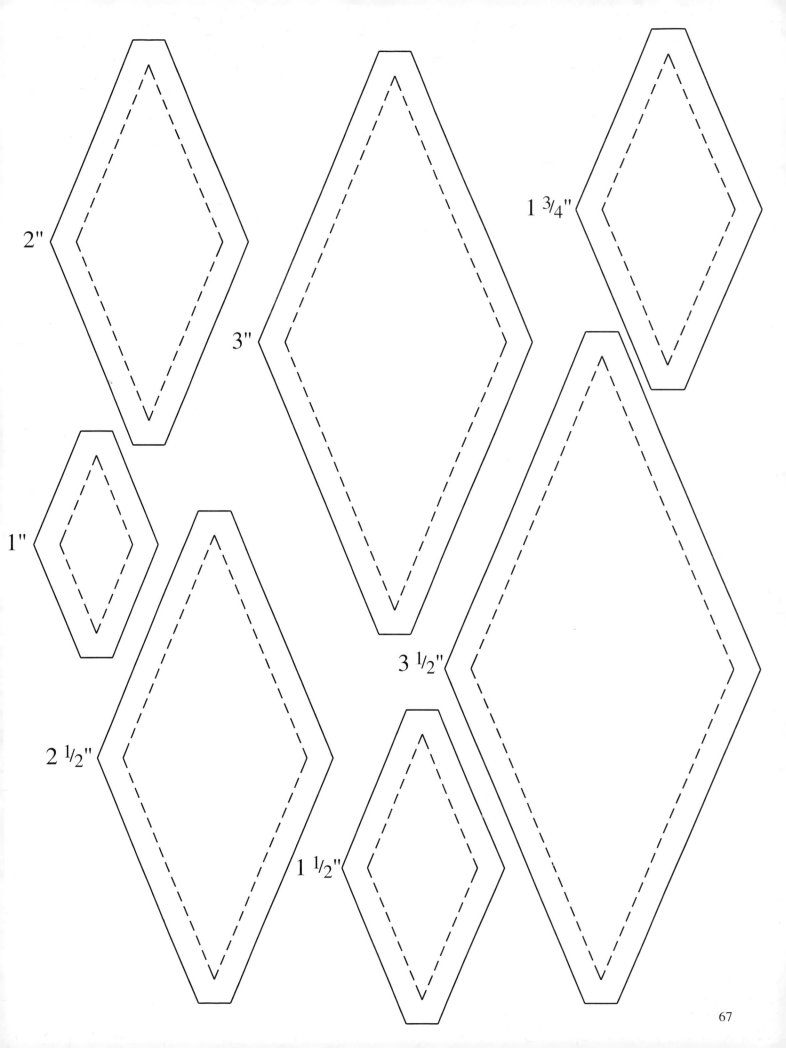

2"

3"

1 ³/₄"

1"

2 ¹/₂"

3 ¹/₂"

1 ¹/₂"

Handy Charts

LeMoyne Star Chart:
6 common block sizes are given with the finished calculation which would show you what size square, half-square triangle, and diamond for the simple LeMoyne Star.

LeMoyne Star Chart

Block Size	Template Size
3"	7/8"
6"	1 3/4"
8"	2 1/3"
9"	2 3/5"
10"	2 9/10"
12"	3 1/2"

Base Grid Unit of Measurement Chart:
I selected four of the more commonly used block sizes which you will find in the first column. Reading across the top you will find the number representing the number of equal divisions across the block. Following the numbers across and down until their rows and columns intersect will give you the unit of measurement used with that size block and that number of equal divisions.

Base Grid Dimensions for Common Block Sizes

Finished Block Size	Number of Equal Divisions					
	3	4	5	6	7	8
6"	2"	1 1/2"	1 1/5"	1"	6/7"	3/4"
9"	3"	2 1/4"	1 4/5"	1 1/2"	1 2/7"	1 1/8"
10"	3 1/3"	2 1/2"	2"	1 2/3"	1 3/7"	1 1/4"
12"	4"	3"	2 2/5"	2"	1 5/7"	1 1/2"

Decimal Equivalents

.03125 = 1/32	.2857 = 2/7	.5625 = 9/16	.78125 = 25/32
.0625 = 1/16	.3 = 3/10	.5714 = 4/7	.8 = 4/5
.09375 = 3/32	.3125 = 5/16	.59375 = 19/32	.8125 = 13/16
.1 = 1/10	.3333 = 1/3	.6 = 3/5	.833 = 5/6
.125 = 1/8	.34375 = 11/32	.625 = 5/8	.84375 = 27/32
.1428 = 1/7	.375 = 3/8	.65625 = 21/32	.8571 = 6/7
.15625 = 5/32	.4 = 2/5	.6666 = 2/3	.875 = 7/8
.1666 = 1/6	.40625 = 13/32	.6875 = 11/16	.9 = 9/10
.1875 = 3/16	.4285 = 3/7	.7 = 7/10	.90625 = 29/32
.2 = 1/5	.4375 = 7/16	.7142 = 5/7	.9375 = 15/16
.21875 = 7/32	.46875 = 15/32	.71875 = 23/32	.96875 = 31/32
.25 = 1/4	.53125 = 17/32	.75 = 3/4	

FINISHED BLOCK SIZE:

This chart would be used to quickly determine what size your finished block would be with certain pre-assigned base grid amounts. To use: read down the column on the left to find the Base Grid amount you wish to work with, next follow across the row at the top to find the number of equal divisions the block has, following across and down until the rows and columns intersect will determine what the block size will finish based on those two factors.

Finished Block Size Based on the Number of Equal Divisions

Assigned Base Grid	3 div	4 div	5 div	6 div	7 div	8 div
1"	3"	4"	5"	6"	7"	8"
1 1/4"	3 3/4"	5"	6 1/4"	7 1/2"	8 3/4"	10"
1 1/2"	4 1/2"	6"	7 1/2"	9"	10 1/2"	12"
1 3/4"	5 1/4"	7"	8 3/4"	10 1/2"	12 1/4"	14"
2"	6"	8"	10"	12"	14"	16"
2 1/4"	6 3/4"	9"	11 1/4"	13 1/2"	15 3/4"	18"
2 1/2"	7 1/2"	10"	12 1/2"	15"	17 1/2"	20"
2 3/4"	8 1/4"	11"	13 3/4"	16 1/2"	19 1/4"	22"
3"	9"	12"	15"	18"	21"	24"

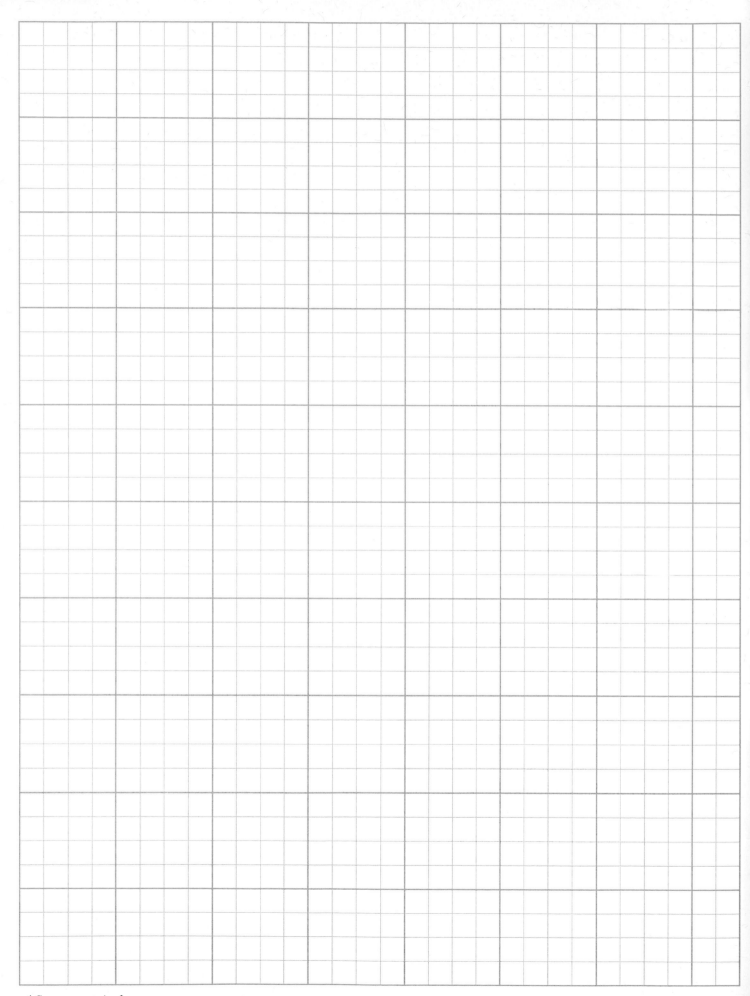

4 Squares per inch

10 Squares per inch

Suggested Reading

Additional inspiration for traditional pieced blocks

Beyer, Jinny. *Patchwork Patterns.* McLean, VA: EPM Publications, Inc., 1979.

Beyer, Jinny. *The Quilter's Album of Blocks and Borders.* McLean, VA: EPM Publications, Inc., 1980.

Hopkins, Mary Ellen. *The It's Okay If You Sit On My Quilt Book.* Santa Monica, CA: ME Publications.

LaBranche, Carol. *Patchwork Pictures.* Pittstown, NJ: The Main Street Press, 1985.

LaBranche, Carol. *A Constellation for Quilters.* Pittstown, NJ: The Main Street Press, 1986.

Martin, Judy. *Judy Martin's Ultimate Book of Quilt Block Patterns.* Denver, CO: Crosley-Griffith Publishing Company, 1988.

Martin, Judy. *Scraps, Blocks & Quilts.* Denver, CO: Crosley-Griffith Publishing Company, 1990.

Block setting ideas—not necessarily the standard fare

Hanson, Joan. *Over 80 Ways to Arrange Your Quilt Blocks.* Bothell, WA: That Patchwork Place, 1993.

Shirer, Marie. *Quilt Settings: A Workbook.* Wheatridge, CO: Moon Over the Mountain Publishing Company, 1989.

In general

Williamson, Darra Duffy. *Sensational Scrap Quilts.* Paducah, KY: American Quilter's Society, 1992.

NOTES

NOTES

NOTES

NOTES